Robert Eden

The sword and gun

A history of the 37th Wis. Volunteer Infantry

Robert Eden

The sword and gun
A history of the 37th Wis. Volunteer Infantry

ISBN/EAN: 9783337197681

Printed in Europe, USA, Canada, Australia, Japan

Cover: Foto ©ninafisch / pixelio.de

More available books at **www.hansebooks.com**

THE

SWORD AND GUN,

A HISTORY OF THE

37th WIS. VOLUNTEER INFANTRY,

From its first Organization to its final Muster Out.

BY MAJOR R. C. EDEN.

MADISON:
ATWOOD & RUBLEE, PRINTERS.
1865.

DEDICATED

TO THE

OFFICERS, NON-COMMISSIONED OFFICERS AND MEN OF THE REGIMENT,

AND

TO THE MEMORY OF THOSE THAT FELL IN THE
SIEGE OF PETERSBURG, 1864–1865,

BY THE AUTHOR.

TABLE OF CONTENTS.

Preface	5
History—Chapter I	7
Chapter II	17
Chapter III	39
Table of Gain and Loss	69
Roster and Muster Rolls	70
List of Deaths	110
Final Roster	117
L'Envoi	118

PREFACE.

I have attempted, in this small volume, to give a true and impartial history of the brief but glorious career of our Regiment. Though called into the field at a late hour, the services of the Regiment have been arduous and severe, in the extreme, and, participating, as it has done, in the last closing scenes of the rebellion, it has shared in the honor and glory of winding up the secession movement.

These memoirs have been mostly compiled from memory, with the assistance of the regimental and company records, and the reminiscences of my brother officers.

For the literary excellence of the work, I claim no merit, as I have not endeavored to accomplish more than the title of the work sets forth: a plain "History of the 37th Regiment Wisconsin Volunteer Infantry." As such a record, it may, I hope, be kindly received among those whose deeds it sets forth; further than that I care little for its fate.

A few years, and the scenes of this rebellion will become misty and indistinct, through the veil of years; a few more, and it will have become a matter of history, minor details and incidents being lost and absorbed in the great broad facts of the period. Then, the author has a hope, a vain one if you will, but springing from the pardonable vanity of a parent in the offspring of his brain, that such records as this will be prized as this generation is passing away, and those who have shared in the stirring events of the time it treats of, may,

—— dying, mention it within their wills,
Bequeathing it, as a rich legacy,
Unto their issue.   [*Julius Cæsar*, Act III, Scene 2.

CHAPTER I.

In the spring of 1864, a call having been made by the President for 500,000 fresh troops, his Excellency, James T. Lewis, issued an order for the raising of a regiment to be designated the 37th Wisconsin Volunteer Infantry.

To Sam. Harriman, of Somerset, St. Croix county, Captain of company A, 30th Wisconsin, was entrusted the charge of raising this regiment, and a commission as Colonel issued to him on the 7th of March.

The work of recruiting was immediately entered into with vigor, and, on the 13th of April, 1864, the first company, (company, B, Capt. R. C. Eden,) was mustered into the service of the United States, at the rendezvous at Madison, by Capt. T. T. Brand, "for three years, unless sooner discharged." On the afternoon of the same day, company C, Capt. John Green, was also mustered in by the same officer, followed on the 12th of the same month by company D, Capt. Alvah Nash, on the 16th by company A, Capt. S. Stevens, on the 18th by company E, Capt. Frank A. Cole, on the 19th by company F, Capt. E. Burnett, on the 3d of May by company G, Capt. W. W Heller, and company H, Capt. Frank T. Hobbs, on the 5th of May by company K, Capt. A. A. Burnett, and on the 6th of the same month by company I, Capt. Geo. A. Beck.

On the 28th of April, companies A, B, C, D, E, and F left Camp Randall, under command of Major Kershaw, and proceeded to Washington, where they arrived on the 1st of May, and were encamped on Arlington Heights, in the neighborhood of the Long Bridge. Colonel Harriman accompanied the regiment as far as Chicago, from which place he returned to Madison, to superintend the organization of the four remaining companies. The journey was accomplished in safety and without the occurrence of any noteworthy incident. On the 17th, the detachment was joined by companies H and I, and arms and accoutrements being at once issued to the men, the instruction of the regiment in the manual and battalion drill was at once proceeded with, with vigor. Lieut. Col. Doolittle, having joined the regiment at Chicago, assumed the command then and there, taking charge of the disciplining and instructing of the eight companies, of which it was then composed.

On the 28th of May, orders were received for the regiment to prepare for the field, and to be ready to march by the next morning. The comfortable "wedge" and "wall" tents in which men and officers had been luxuriating and gaining their first experience of camp life were, accordingly, turned in to the Regimental Quartermaster, and the fragmentary and disjointed dwellings, known to the polite world as shelter tents, or *tents d'abri*, but known amongst soldiers as *pup tents*, were issued in their stead. All extra baggage was disposed of, and the comforts of civilized life bid adieu to, "for three years unless sooner discharged."

At daylight, on the morning of the 29th, we took up

our line of march for Alexandria, thus entering on our first campaign. The morning was sunny and clear, and as the sun gained power, became unpleasantly warm, and a source of no little distress to men unused to marching and the encumbrance of gun, knapsack and accoutrements, as ours were. About ten o'clock, we arrived in the suburbs of Alexandria, where we rested for an hour or two, awaiting orders as to our further disposition.

The transports on which we were to embark for White House Landing, on the Pamunkey River, the then base of supplies of the Army of Virginia, had arrived the night previous and were then engaged in taking on board a large herd of cattle, which was to form part of their live freight, and we were accordingly ordered into camp on the banks of the river where we remained till 5 o'clock on the afternoon of the 30th. The work of embarking the troops was then commenced, and our Regiment was divided into three divisions, which were distributed as follows: Companies B and E were assigned to the propeller *S. Cloud*, under command of Capt. Eden, of company B; the propeller *Andrew Harder* carried companies A, C, D and F, under command of Lieut. Col. Doolittle, while Capt. Hobbs took command of the remainder of the detachment on board of the *Charles Osgood*.

With the exception of the *Harder's* grounding on a sand bank just above Mt. Vernon, and nearly involving the *Cloud*, which came to her assistance, in a like catastrophe, no incident, unpleasant or otherwise, occurred to mar the tranquility of our passage down the Potomac.

We made a pleasant run down Chesapeake Bay, and the morning of the second of June found us, after a close escape from grounding on York Spit,—a long narrow point of sand off the mouth of York River,—preparing to anchor off Yorktown to wait for a pilot to conduct us up the intricate navigation of the York and Pamunkey Rivers. The original intention had been for us to follow up the *Harder*, the only vessel in the squadron that carried a government pilot, but owing to her neglecting to display a proper signal, during the night, we had lost sight of her and were consequently left to our own resources.

Our preparations for anchoring were yet in course of completion when the pilot was seen, coming out of Yorktown, and the squadron was again headed up the York River. About noon we passed West Point, an insignificant collection of small dwellings, situated on a long point of land between the York and Pamunkey rivers, and just at their junction. From this point to White House Landing the Pamunkey is, perhaps, as crooked a river as can be found in the United States. The channel, however, is straight and deep, running between low, flat marshes occasionally relieved with high, steep banks and well wooded bluffs, capital points for guerrilla operations.

Rumors were rife as to the exploits of these gentry, in this neighborhood, and the several divisions of the detachment received orders to load, many of them then performing that operation for the first time. The size of our squadron, however, and the presence of several "tinclads" and "double enders," those "restless wanderers of the *deeps*" and shallows, tended no doubt to awe the bushwhackers and keep them on their best behavior.

At any rate the Thirty-Seventh passed along, unmolested and unmolesting, except when an insubordinate recruit would insist on trying the range of Springfield or (contraband) Colt on sundry and divers vagabond members of the porcine tribe, that seemed to lead an aimless and unsatisfactory life, on the banks of the Pamunkey. And so the long summer's day passed away, with the hot perpendicular rays of the sun shining down on our bare decks, unchecked by awning or shelter of any kind, frying the pitch out of the deck seams and reducing the tar in the rigging to the consistency of molasses and leaving about as pleasant an impression on the incautious hands of those who ventured to touch strand or stay. But "all things come to an end," says the wise man, and so even will a long hot summer day, if it is passed on board a crowded transport, with a scarcity of standing, sitting or lying room, a still greater scarcity of drinkable water, and an utter absence of anything at all approaching to comfort.

About 5 P. M., a sudden turn in the river brings us in sight of the chimneys of what once was the White House, from which the landing, which is for the present to be our destination, takes its name. A few more throbbing, restless pulsations of our propeller's wheel, and its action grows fainter and slower as, amidst a crowd of steamers, propellers, tug-boats, schooners, barges, scows, skiffs, and all the crowd of craft incident to a base of supplies, we work our way up to the landing. Again a few more revolutions of the wheel, a jar and a crash accompanied by a few nautical expletives, and we grind alongside of a sutler's barge, blundering down stream, without any apparent directing power or any definite object in view; till at length one of the never-resting, spiteful looking, everwatchful tug-boats darts out from some labyrinth of hulls, pounces on it and drags it away, awkward and clumsy and apparently remonstrating and resisting to the last, into its proper and designated mooring place. Then a sudden cessation of the, to all appearance, endless jar and throb of the screw, a tangled web of heaving-lines flying through the air, a deafening roar as the pent up steam raises the valve and comes tumbling out at the escape pipe and eddies and whirls about as if for pure joy at its liberation from restraint; a few more double-shotted nautical expletives, a vast amount of veering and hauling on heavy hawsers and the transports are made fast and our voyage ended.

But, if the confusion on the river was great, that on the shore was certainly, to all appearances, much greater. Mule drivers, addressing their jaded teams by every soothing and endearing epithet in the well stocked vocabulary of their class, and the mules replying in their scarcely less intelligible, and much less profane, dialect; long wagon trains, coming and going in every direction; colored laborers, rolling barrels on to every bodies' toes, their own included, and becoming the patient recipients of remarks objurgatory of their eyes and limbs, therefor. Long lines of stretchers loaded with wounded being carried on board two large hospital steamers, loading for Washington; ambulances arriving from the front, with fresh cases; orderlies, hot and dusty, riding, walking, or running in every direction; clouds of dust and smoke, from camp fires and steamboats; shouting, braying, swearing, yelling, (from the mules) whistling from the steamboats, combined altogether to form a scene of noise and confusion, to which the grand finale at the tower of Babel was, by comparison, nothing but a quiet assemblage of sober and well behaved mechanics. Threading our way, with no little difficulty, through this motley assemblage, we at length gained a quiet and comparatively secluded spot where we were, much to our relief, ordered to camp; and this we, nothing loth, proceeded at once to do.

Here we remained, guarding prisoners and picketing along the line of the Richmond railroad, till the 10th of June; here we, for the first time, heard the sound of shotted guns, as the terrible battle of the 3d of June surged and roared, nearly twenty miles away, in our front. And all that night, and part of the 4th, the long trains of ambulances, each bearing its ghastly load of bleeding and suffering men, rolled through our camp, giving us our first insight into the horrors of war, in which we were soon to take an active part. Here, too, we had a first insight into the heroism and patience under suffering of. those who form our armies; numbers of slightly wounded, or, who at least were not absolutely prevented from traveling by the loss of limbs, came straggling through our camps, many only just able to limp along; some with hands or arms bandaged; others with ugly cuts on the head or face, their hair all matted and tangled, soaked with blood and clogged with the dust of the road, hungry, thirsty, weary and suffering, but uttering no complaints, and patient and cheerful under it all.

And in the Depot Hospital at the landing we had an opportunity of witnessing the heroic and charitable part the women of America were taking in the war. No matter how ragged or dirty the sufferer, how hideous or revolting the wound, alive in many instances with maggots, and in every form of putrefaction and mortification; no matter what nation or country the patient belonged to; woman's kind, ministering hand was there, to wash the festering wound, to bathe the toil-worn feet, to comb the matted locks, hold the cooling draught to the parched lips, or to receive the last words that fell from them e'er they were closed forever. And this without reward or hire, or expectation of it, their only recompense the consciousness of obeying the mandate that makes charity our duty, their only reward the knowledge that they are aiding to maintain the government and preserve the integrity of the stars and stripes.

But we linger too long around White House Landing and scenes, which, though then novel and strange to us, have since become a part of our every day life. On the 10th of June, we were dispatched from the base as guard to a supply train, under charge of Capt. Alex. Samuels, of the 5th Wisconsin, which was on its way to the front at Cool Arbor, or Cold Harbor, as it is sometimes written. Much dispute has been held, as to tho orthography and derivation of the name of this place, it being called indiscriminately Cool Arbor, Cold Harbor, Cool Harbor, and Coal Harbor. The first would, however, seem to be the most appropriate designation, as there is no Harbor, nor any navigable stream to convert into one, within ten miles of the place. I have been informed by a Virginian who is acquainted with the locality, that the name originated as follows:

Cool Arbor, which is nothing more than a large farm house or tavern on one of the main highways leading to Richmond, was originally built by an Englishman, as a place of summer resort for the citizens of that place, and named by him Cool Arbor, from its pleasant and shady location. The proverbial (H)english disregard of the use of the aspirate probably converted the second word of the name into Harbor, and a broad provincial dialect would easily effect the transition from Cool to Coal or Cold. Its claim to either title is now a poor one, for trees and farm have both alike disappeared, and in the words of the poet, "*pericrunt etiam ruinæ*"—the very ruins are gone.

At this place we arrived in safety after a long and tedious march of nearly twenty miles, along a heavy, sandy road plentifully bestrewn with dead mules, wagons broken or stuck in the swamps, and abandoned, and all the *debris* usually to be seen on the line of communication between a large army and its base. Our march was only marked by the incidents common to such a trip; an overturned wagon now and then to be righted, or a brokendown mule to be led to the roadside and shot; a vexatious delay of perhaps half an hour, to make some repair to harness or wheels, and then a forced march for a mile or two to catch up with the rest of the train.

To any one that has never tried it, the task of guarding a wagon train may, perhaps, be recommended as an amusement, on the score of novelty, but we hardly think it is one that can be either pleasantly or profitably followed up, as a steady trade.

On arriving at Cool Arbor we were assigned to the 1st Brigade, 3d Division of the 9th, or Burnside's, Army Corps, temporarily attached to the Army of the Potomac, though in reality belonging to no army in particular, and better known amongst military men as "Burnside's Traveling Menagerie," so called, not from the heterogeneous collection composing it, but from the wandering nature of the service it had been engaged in since its organization. Our Division Commander was Brig. Gen. O. B. Willcox, of the regular army, since promoted to be Brevet Major General, and our Brigade Commander, Brig. Gen. John F. Hartrauft, afterwards Major General of Volunteers, commanding the Third Provisional Division of the 9th Army Corps.

On the morning of the 12th of June we were ordered from the position we held on the flank, into the front line of works, where we had the pleasure of listening to the music of shot and shell, and of inspecting a rebel line of fortifications, for the first time.

CHAPTER II.

THE SIEGE OF PETERSBURG.

On the evening of the 12th of June, just as we had settled ourselves down, to pass, as best we might, our first night in the trenches, and amid the roar of artillery and the uncouth yells of the combatants, to snatch a few hours' much needed sleep we received orders to pack up and be ready to march an hour after sundown, to exercise the utmost caution in our movements, and to allow no talking nor rattling of arms, accoutrements or equipage to be heard, bayonets to be unfixed and arms carried at the trail

And it was so. Quietly and stealthily on that still June evening the whole Army of the Potomac stole away from under the dark sombre pine woods where it laid encamped, and commenced its flank march on Petersburg. Our road, for the first ten or twelve miles, lay in the direction of White House Landing, and, except that we kept to the fields, the roads being occupied by our trains and artillery, was almost a repetition of our route from the Landing to the front.

Just short of White House, however, we turned sharp to the right and kept away for Baltimore and Kent Cross Roads and Charles City Court House At the last named place we were delayed some twelve hours by the 2d Corps supply train failing to connect, thus affording us a rest, which, however much it may have disconcerted the plans of the Lieutenant General, was very acceptable to the men, on whom the long and rapid marching was beginning to tell.

We resumed our march about an hour before sundown on the afternoon of the 15th, and at dark were crossing the James River on the pontoons laid over it at Harrison's Landing. Our course then lay along the left bank of the river and parallel to it, leaving City Point on our right and bringing us up to the front of the city of Petersburg, about 4 o'clock on the afternoon of the 16th of June.

Our sufferings on this day's march, from heat, thirst and fatigue combined, were severe in the extreme, but, to the credit of our regiment, with the exception of one or two cases of sun stroke, not a man fell out, or was missing when we arrived at our final destination.

We had hardly halted and commenced preparations for supper when we were ordered to move on to support a charge about to be made by the 4th, or colored division, of our corps, and so marched about a mile further, formed line of battle in a piece of pine woods and awaited orders. But a short time had elapsed before a confused cheer, or rather yell, in our front followed by a dropping fire of musketry and a few rounds from the artillery told that the ball had opened and that our turn might arrive any minute. The firing, however, gradually died away without our services being required, and we shortly learned that the sable gentry had been successful and had carried the first line of the defences of Petersburg. Supposing that our services would not be further required, we proceeded to prepare our long deferred and much desired supper, but hardly had the scent of the coffee—the great stand-by and panacea of the soldier—become perceptible to our expectant senses, before the unwelcome order came for us again to move and hold the line of works the colored troops had taken. With many a sigh, the tempting decoction of the Arabian herb was consigned to the sacred soil of Virginia—in plain English we threw away our coffee—and with many an insubordinate growl and execration on the "exigencies of the service," we started for our new scene of labors. A few solid shot and shell, and one or two rounds of case and canister were pitched at us as we moved up to the works, which beyond creating some slight consternation, did no damage whatever, and, having occupied the old line of rebel works, wo passed the night without molestation and in comparative peace.

Early on the morning of the 17th June, the brigade was formed in line of battle, in a ravine, preparatory to charging a line of works, extending from the Bagster Road almost to Hare Hill, the future site of Fort Steadman. This line of works was situated in the middle of a field of corn, then just in the tassel, on the crest of a ridge or slight elevation, and was built in the shape of the letter V, the apex of the line being towards the rear. To the right and left of the line were batteries, and another in a narrow section of pine woods covered the centre of the line. Though not very strongly manned, the work was a heavy one, and from its commanding position and the heavy enfilading fire that could be brought to bear on almost any part of it, not by any means an easy one to carry. Our line was however formed, and we stood there, the hot bright sun almost blinding us and beating the dry sand under our feet, till it almost blistered them, awaiting the orders to commence our first battle. A desultory fire was being kept up by a line of skirmishers and sharpshooters entrenched a little in advance of our line and a round of spherical case or canister would occasionally come whistling over our heads, spattering sharply and viciously through the timber close in our rear and making the limbs and splinters fly far and wide. At length the preparations were all made, and with beating hearts we waited for the word; it came at last: "Forward, double quick! charge!" a wild, loud cheer, rolls along from one end to the other of the brigade, a sudden trampling of feet breaks in on the comparative quiet of the summer's morning, a few seconds and the line of works in our front becomes wreathed in smoke, as we mount a low bank which had hitherto concealed it from our view;—an angry roar from the batteries in the woods in front of us, and an hailstorm of shot, shell, grape, canister, and minie balls screaming through the air above and around us and throwing up clouds of dust, as they strike the sand in every direction. till the whole battle field is obscured by a heavy cloud of dust and smoke through which the rebel works in front of us and their truculent looking butternut defenders are barely discernible. And through it all the wild cheering yell of our boys as they pant and struggle on through the deep sand, which fills mouth and nostrils, almost suffocating us; the crash and roar of cannon and musketry, the bursting of shells, the whiz of the missiles as they pass, the cries of the wounded as they roll over in their agony, all blended and mingling together, yet each sound distinct and clear as if the only one to break the stillness of the summer air. But no words can paint a battle any more than can canvas portray its details, which only those who have participated in can appreciate or understand. On we go,

> "On, on, through the hell-fire of shrapnel and shell
> On without faltering, right on with a yell,"

till we see the scowling, wolfish looking faces of the rebels in their works, till their fire slackens, till we can see the artillerymen working the guns of the battery on our left limbering up their pieces and starting to the rear, till the right of their line breaks slowly from their works and retires to the rear.

Then comes an order "half wheel to the right," a wavering confused movement along the whole line, a yell of derision from the Rebels, a sudden recommencement of their fire; and, with victory within its grasp, the brigade falls back on the line of works they lately left confident of victory, shattered and broken and leaving hundreds of its numbers on the field.

From whom the order came directing the movement to the right has never, I believe, been satisfactorily established, but to this order, exposing the whole brigade, as it did, to a most severe enfilading fire, may be attributed the failure of the charge and the heavy loss sustained by the brigade. Our leading files were close up to the works, the Rebels were withdrawing their men and guns, and had we but been allowed to go right ahead, we should have taken the whole and suffered much less loss than we did. Had we done so, our entrance into Petersburg that afternoon would have been easily accomplished, as the troops opposed to us were nothing but the Petersburg Reserves, raw militia, and few in number.

Our regiment suffered severely in this its first day's fight. Major Kershaw was shot through the legs; Lieut. Colonel Doolittle was slightly wounded in the shoulder and had his shoulder strap torn off by a piece of a shell; Lieut. Earl, Co. B, received a gunshot wound which caused his death shortly afterwards; Lieut. F. B. Riddle, Co. C, was mortally wounded, and Capt. Green received a slight contusion from a piece of shell.

In this engagement Serg't Greene, of company C, the Regimental Color Bearer, was shot through both legs by a grape shot, in the early part of the fight; unable to walk and fearful lest the colors entrusted to his charge, should fall into the hands of the enemy, he rolled up the flag on the staff and seizing this in his teeth, drew himself off the field and behind the works into a place of safety. Such unselfish heroism is deserving the highest commendation, though poor Greene lived barely long enough to know that his courageous act was known and appreciated. Our loss in killed and wounded in this battle amounted to 138 of which number 44 were killed on the field and 10 died from the effects of their wounds.

I do not suppose that a more disheartened and, for the time, broken down set of men ever met together, than the scattered fragments of our regiment when we collected in the ravine after our ill-fated charge on the first day of the battle of Petersburg. Our men had been marched for four successive days and nights, had had little or no sleep for five, and been on short rations for the same period. To this may be added that depressed feeling, the natural sequence of great excitement, which always follows a battle, even if successful; the loss of so many of our number, and a feeling that would creep in—that there had been a blunder, somewhere.

We remained in the ravine for an hour or two, getting rest and refreshment, of both of which we stood in much need. Towards night, however, we were ordered forward to support the Second Division who had advanced their works some way up the field. We accordingly took possession of a partially constructed breastwork on the edge of the ravine, and after an hour or two employed in further completing and strengthening our defences, lay down to get what rest we could to prepare us for what the morrow might have in store for us. We slept that night, without rocking, and a heavy fire that the enemy opened on our lines during the night, hardly awakened us. At daylight we were roused up and ordered to advance in line of battle, with two companies deployed as skirmishers, which order, however, was afterwards modified by the 8th Michigan being deployed along the whole Brigade front.

We advanced steadily and slowly over the scene of yesterday's battle and found the line of works for which we had then contended unoccupied, except by the rebel dead, who were pretty thickly piled up all along the works. We entered the woods I have before mentioned as being in the rear of the defenses, in which we found traces of a large camp, which had evidently been abandoned in great haste. Muster rolls and other military records, more or less complete, were scattered round in every direction, cooking utensils and a variety of eatables lay round every where, forming, with worn out clothing and accoutrements and the remains of the huts and tents, a lively picture of confusion and ruin.

A brisk fire on the skirmish line showed that we were fast approaching the scene of action, and on reaching the edge of the timber we were ordered to build breastworks and await the arrival of Gen. Bartlett's command on our right. The day was clear and bright, and, owing to a light northerly breeze, not unpleasantly warm. Our boys soon threw up a light line of works and lay down under the shade of the pines to rest.

The situation was a picturesque one not devoid of a certain solemnity. The light breeze hummed through the pines overhead, with a pleasant dreamy sound; before us lay a field of oats, waving and undulating in alternate light and shade as the soft breath of the summer wind passed over it; far off on the right the distant spires of Petersburg showed faint and indistinct through the soft blue haze; on our left a cloud of dark, black smoke curled lazily up over the tree tops, and dropped gently away to leeward from where a large cotton factory had been fired by the rebels in their retreat. The air was alive with the hum of insects and the chirp of birds, and in the trees, on the left of our regiment, a mocking bird was whistling, softly but clearly. It was a strange scene, the long lines of faces, the subdued murmur of conversation, broken only by an occasional shot from the skirmish line, sounding strangely distant and unreal, and the flickering shadow of the pine boughs falling at times on some sunburnt face, with a grave fixed look on it, which showed how the thoughts were then traveling back over hundreds of miles to some spot in the far-off North where the loved ones lay, little conscious of the fate of their nearest and dearest.

On many faces there a darker shadow than that of the pine boughs was soon to fall forever, and a brighter and more lasting glory than that of the sun's rays, as the swaying boughs moved aside and let in the gleaming light. For many there, their last sun had arisen, and the fitful slumber that now from time to time drooped their eyelids was but the prelude to the "sleep that knows no waking"

But our thoughts were soon recalled to the realities of the occasion by the order to advance, and under a sharp fire of cannon and musketry we pressed on across the oat-field towards a line of works just discernible, ahead of us. On we went, steadily and unwaveringly, halting only once to reform the line which had become somewhat broken from the uneven nature of the ground over which we were advancing. Forward! again with a cheer, and we see their skirmishers falling back on their main line of battle; forward a few steps more, and a wide trench unexpectedly opens before us—it is a deep cut on the Norfolk and Petersburg railroad. A momentary pause as we catch in a telegraph wire cunningly stretched on stakes and hid in the long rank grass on the edge of the cut, and a withering volley sweeps the top of the cut, and numbers roll down its steep sides to find a grave in the muddy ditches on the side of the track. Up the steep bank, on the opposite side, the fragments of our brigade try, once more, to charge, but the fire that meets them is too heavy, and they fall back under the protection of the sides of the cut.

Twice again they attempt it, and twice again they are compelled to fall back, leaving many of their number behind on each successive charge. And now, on our right, the enemy's sharpshooters have got into position and, firing along the whole length of the cut, pick off a man at every shot. Capt. Stevens, of Co. A, is mortally wounded, and 2d Lieut. Lowber, of the same company, receives a ball through his fore-arm, thus leaving that company without an officer. And now the enemy are seen getting a battery into position on a height commanding the whole of our position. None of our artillery has yet come up to support us, and our position if not a critical, is at least, a most anxious one. But soon the sharp crack of a Napoleon is heard in our rear and the solid shot hums along over our heads and sends up a cloud of dust and splinters as it strikes where the rebels are trying to build an earthwork, and Capt. Romer, of the 34th N. Y., has got his guns into position, and with a few well directed shots, shells the rebels away from their covert. The crack of those Napoleons was a thoroughly welcome sound to us all, for it gave evidence that we were not all alone nor without backers, which, as the troops on our right and left did not connect with us, appeared at one time to be the case.

And so the 18th of June, a day memorable in the history of battles, as the anniversary of Waterloo and Bunker Hill, wore to a close, and as the welcome shades of night drew in around us, fresh troops taking our place, we fell back to the woods we had left in the morning, with sadly diminished numbers, thoroughly wearied and exhausted.

Our loss in this day's battle, though not so severe as in the charge of the preceding day was, nevertheless, very heavy in proportion to the number of men engaged. In company A, Capt. Stevens was mortally, and 2d Lieut. D. A. Lowber, severely wounded, and company B lost its 2d Lieut. N. S. Davison, shot through the shoulder. Our total loss in killed and wounded was 103, of which number 20 were killed on the field or died of wounds, and 83 wounded, making with the casualties of yesterday, an aggregate of 64 killed and 186 wounded. Total loss 250 out of 400.

We remained in the position to which we retired on the night of the 18th June, till the evening of the 20th of the same month, when we again occupied the front line of works to the right of our previous position on an eminence known as Hare Hill, so called from the owner of the plantation on which it is situated, and which was afterwards chosen as the site for Fort Steadman.

We remained here till the morning of the 22d, when we returned to our old position, on the Norfolk and Petersburg R. R., where we remained doing picket and fatigue duty, exposed day and night to a heavy fire of artillery and musketry, till the 10th of July. On the 28th of June, Lieut. David Prutsman, of company D, was killed by one of the enemy's sharpshooters while sitting at breakfast, in the trenches, and our losses in all up to this period amounted to 286 rank and file. In addition to this the extreme heat of the weather and the confinement to which they were subjected in the trenches, had caused our previously well thinned ranks to be reduced still lower by sickness. The position of the regiment, all through the hot summer months was, indeed, anything but enjoyable, lying on the dusty, sandy ground, exposed to the full power of the sun's rays by day and the damp chilly dews by night; obliged to remain in a recumbent position, where to raise a cap above the breast work was to make it the target for half a dozen sharpshooters; water, even for drinking purposes, hard to get and poor at that, so that when on the 10th of July we were ordered to the rear, it was hailed by all as a respite from prison.

After a week's rest, during which, for fear I suppose that the men might get lazy for want of work, they were kept busy cutting and carrying material for abattis, the 37th was, on the 17th July, again ordered into the trenches, where they remained till the morning of the 30th of July, the day of the battle of Cemetery Hill, or as it is generally called the "Mine Fort."

This Fort, which was one of the strongest of the enemy's works, was situated on a hill a little to the right, and in front of our position, immediately in front of the cemetery at Blandford, one of the suburbs of Petersburg. A mine had been driven under the direction of Colonel Pleasant of the 48th Penn. Vol. Inf., from the rear of the Horse-shoe, where our regiment lay, under this fort, had been charged and primed, and was to be exploded at daylight on the morning of the 30th. Immediately on the explosion of the mine, the 9th corps was to advance on the crater and, taking advantage of the confusion and consternation excited, endeavor to break and hold the enemy's line. On eminences to the right and left of Cemetery Hill were forts which commanded it, and from which a severe enfilading fire could be directed on the fort itself, and an error in the plan of attack seems to have been the neglect of having a force ready to attack and, if possible, capture these works simultaneously with the assault on the main work, for, had they been captured or their fire silenced, there is no doubt but that a permanent lodgment would have been effected in the main line of the defences of Petersburg.

From the report of the Committee on the Conduct of the War, the blame of the failure of the whole plan, in consequence of this blunder, seems to be attributed to General Meade, and it would certainly seem to be an act of negligence on his part, with the force he had at his disposal, to leave these important points unmolested.

The original arrangement had been to explode the mine at half past four A. M, and for the assaulting column to advance immediately, but, owing to a fault in the fuse, it was nearly 6 o'clock before the explosion took place. At that time a vast column of smoke mingled with earth, fragments of guns and platforms, logs, sand-bags, gabions and human beings shot towering into the air to an immense height, gradually subsiding again and followed immediately by a dull, smothered roar which shook the ground for miles round, and was said to have been felt even to City Point. A pause, in which one might count, perhaps a dozen beats at the wrist, and 85 pieces of heavy artillery opened almost simultaneously on the rebel lines. The enemy was not slow in replying, and soon the light artillery and musketry chimed in, making the noise completely deafening, and the very ground under our feet to vibrate. From 6 till 12 this hellish uproar continued unabated at which time it commenced to slacken, till, by four o'clock, it died away, and, as the last of our troops fell back from the crater, the battle of July 30th was at an end.

On the explosion of the mine, the rebels fled from their works on each side of it, panic stricken, but, owing to some unaccountable blunder, this panic was not taken advantage of, as it might, and should have been, and the word to advance not being given, for some minutes, time was given the rebels to recover from the consternation into which the explosion, thoroughly unlooked for by them, had thrown them.

The word was given, at last; the charge was made, and the crater of the exploded mine occupied by our troops at an inconsiderable loss. Col. Harriman, assisted by Adjutant C. I. Miltimore and men from different regiments, succeeded in extricating two of the rebel guns from the ruins of the fort, and turning them against their late possessors.

The rebels had, by this time, however, recovered from their first panic, which had led them to hastily and precipitately abandon the works on each side the fort, and were forming in line of battle for the purpose of recapturing the ruins of the works, and, to cover the attack, were pouring in a tremendous enfilading fire from the two forts on the right and left. Reinforcements were sent into the crater from time to time, but no orders being given for an attack on either of the flanking works, the crater had, by this time, become densely packed with troops, and the explosion having completely leveled the parapet, they were left almost entirely without protection, and the whole place soon become a perfect slaughter house. The position was held, however, till about 4 o'clock in the afternoon, when, the rebels having advanced near enough to plant their colors on the outside of the works, and our men being unable to accomplish anything or to hold the works without immense loss of life, orders were given for them to fall back to our main line, which was accordingly done.

In this engagement, out of two hundred and fifty men who went into action in the morning, only 95 remained to answer their names at roll-call that evening. Capt. A. A. Burnett, of company K, received a wound in the head, from the effects of which he died on the 18th of August; Capt. Frank A. Cole, received a severe wound in the hip, which necessitated an operation which proved fatal; Lieuts. Atwell, G; L. U. Beal, E, and George D. Mc-Dill, K, also received wounds which incapacitated them from further service, and Lieuts. Munger, D, and Holmes, G, were taken prisoners.

On the evening of the battle, the regiment was relieved from the front line and allowed to withdraw to the rear, where it remained, doing fatigue duty, till the 19th of August.

On the night of the 19th, the whole regiment was sent out on fatigue, the work in which they were engaged being the erection of a large fort, afterwards named Fort Schenckl, on the Jerusalem Plankroad.

On returning to camp at daylight, next morning, orders were found awaiting us, "to strike tents and get ready to march at once." This was no very welcome order for men who had been hard at work all night, part of the time exposed to a rather brisk artillery fire; but there was no help for it, the rest of the brigade had already started, and so after a hasty cup of coffee and a half hour's nap we started out to overtake the command. After a long and tedious march through rain and mud, made at a rapid rate, we caught up with the remainder of the brigade, which had moved out before daylight, near the Yellow Tavern, and after a short rest were ordered into action to repel an attack of the enemy on our front line. The rebels fell back as we advanced, being driven by us through the woods, till, gaining an open place and receiving reinforcements, they once more made a stand, and the 57th was ordered to take up a new position further to the left, which they did, and held the same till dark, having lost ten killed and wounded during the battle. During the night of the 19th and throughout the whole of the 20th, the regiment was moved, from point to point, as the enemy massed his troops in different positions, in attempting to regain possession of the Weldon road.

At an early hour on the 21st of August, the regiment was set to work building a line of entrenchments across the Weldon railroad, facing towards the rear of our main line of works. The works were hardly completed before a determined and combined attack was made by the enemy on three different points, simultaneously, for the purpose of regaining possession of the railroad. The 37th was ordered up to support the 19th New York battery, which was in position on the extreme left of our line, and which was suffering severely from the effects of a rapid and well directed fire which was being directed against them from a rebel battery in their rear and to the left. In performing this duty the 37th suffered severely, losing 10 killed and 25 wounded, but succeeding in finally compelling the enemy to withdraw his guns.

Till the 25th the men were kept hard at work doing picket and guard duty, and building breastworks and fortifications commanding the Weldon railroad and its approaches. On that day, however, we were once more ordered to march, our destination being Reams' Station, where the 2d Corps was engaged and in need of support. On approaching the scene of action we soon found strong presumptive evidence of the truth of this position, the road, for several miles, being thickly lined with stragglers wearing the clover leaf, the distinguishing badge of the 2d Corps, and showing that an active retrograde move was in progression. A part of our brigade was kept to do provost guard duty and stop and re-assemble the stragglers as best they might, while the rest, including the 37th, pushed on and covered the retreat of the 2d Corps, holding the enemy in check till dark, when we fell back within our lines and slept on our arms that night.

On the 27th a new line of works was constructed and a new camp formed near Blick Station, where the time was passed till the 24th of September in guard and picket duty. On the 29th the regiment moved to the neighborhood of the Yellow Tavern, where Colonel Harriman assumed command of the brigade, now 1st Brig. 1st Div.

9th A. C. and Major Kershaw, who had partially recovered from the effects of the wounds he received on the 17th of June, and had rejoined the regiment, took command of the same. The brigade marched to the neighborhood of Poplar Grove Church where it was formed as reserve to the second brigade, which was about assault to the enemy's works defending the South Side Railroad and which were distant about a mile and a half.

In the charge, the 2d brigade was repulsed and, retiring in disorder, threw part of the 1st brigade into confusion; a battery also which had been sent up to check the advance of the enemy, retreated rapidly to the rear, as the enemy advanced from out of the wood, thus materially adding to the confusion. The 37th fell back to where the temporary shelter of a fence enabled them to reform their line of battle, and by a heavy and well sustained fire, repulsed several attacks of the enemy, and held the position till reinforcements arrived and the imminent defeat was thus rendered a victory. The same night the regiment went into camp on the Pegram farm where they constructed a heavy line of works strongly protected by forts and a line of abattis. The losses of the regiment in this successive series of battles amounted in all to 25 killed and 75 wounded, and gained it a reputation which it has maintained untarnished to the end. We remained in camp on the Pegram farm and in that vicinity, occupied in picket and fatigue duty till the 28th of October, when we took part in the reconnoissance in force made in the direction of Thatcher's Run. Our loss in this affair was very trifling, only two men being wounded, one very slightly. We advanced about three miles, meeting little or no opposition, and having entrenched and remained one night in the immediate presence of the enemy, we fell back to our former position on the morning of the 29th. During this movement Adjt. C. T. Miltimore was wounded whilst on the picket line.

In the latter part of November, the 9th corps was moved from the extreme left to the extreme right of the Army of the Potomac, its left resting on the Weldon R. R. and its right on the Appomattox; this brought the 1st Brigade back to their old station in front of the Mine or Crater Fort, with the 37th Wis. and 109th N. Y. in reserve in the woods, in the rear of the main line.

Our time here was fully occupied in building houses for the winter, standing picket, doing guard and fatigue duty more or less exposed to the enemy's fire, day and night.

On the 8th of December the 37th, in company with the 109th N. Y. were ordered to move to the rear and report to Brevet Col. Robinson, commanding Provisional Brigade. We moved out soon after dark on a bitter cold night, a cutting north-east wind sweeping over the bare surface of the country with a chill that went to the marrow. All that night and the next day and night, when a mingled storm of rain and snow set in, as if to cap the climax and add what little was wanting, of making our situation as uncomfortable as possible, we remained on a bare open common, without any tents, a good many without blankets, and with nothing at hand with which to build a fire.

The Sanitary Commission, with its well known generosity, sent down a pair of woolen mittens and a cup of hot milk punch for each man in the brigade, on the evening of the second day, which added materially to our comfort and rendered our situation somewhat more endurable.

At length, at about 3 o'clock of the afternoon of the third day, the orders came to march. It was drawing towards the close of a dull, raw winter's day as our men, stiff and cold with exposure and want of rest, started wearily off down the Jerusalem Plank Road. The road was almost knee deep in half frozen mud and sleet, the broken planks lay round in every direction, and as we blundered on through the darkness that, accompanied by a drizzling rain, soon fell on us, many "a curse not loud but deep" was vented on Virginia, her roads and her rebels. Once, and once only did we rest that night, and daylight, or as much of it as could struggle through a dull, leaden looking sky, found us at the end of our march, at Hawkin's Tavern, on the Nottoway River, the scene of the defeat of Kautz and Wilson in their raid during the summer of '63. And here, for the first time, we learned the nature and object of our expedition.

The second and fifth corps had started off on a raid along the line of the Weldon R. R. which they had struck at Jarrett's Station, and had torn up and destroyed the track from that point to the North Carolina line, burning the bridge over the Meherrin River, and pushing on, almost to Weldon. Our mission was to reinforce them and protect their rear, on the homeward march, if the disposition of the enemy's force should seem to menace their safety, and we were ordered to wait at Hawkins' till their rear had passed.

About 3 o'clock the Second Corps passed through our camp and immediately afterwards the Provisional Brigade was put in motion and followed them at a rapid rate. About two miles from Hawkin's we passed through the midst of the 2d corps, camped on each side the road, but no orders were given us to halt and our command was pushed on, without a halt and without a rest, until the thirty miles between us and camp were accomplished. This was the severest marching we ever undertook, the distance being accomplished in about seven hours by men in heavy marching order, carrying sixty rounds ammunition and four days rations, besides their knapsacks and accoutrements, and chilled and stiffened by exposure to three days and nights very inclement weather. On our return, in retaliation for the murder of two of its number by citizens of Sussex county, the 2d corps fired every house and building along the line of march, from the Nottoway river to our rear line of works, in front of Petersburg, drove off large numbers of oxen, sheep, pigs, horses, mules, &c., and brought in with them a large number of negroes.

After our return to the inside of our lines in front of Petersburg, we remained for two days in a temporary camp, in rear of the Jones House, after which we returned to our old camp on the Baxter Road, where we remained in winter quarters till the opening of the campaign of '65.

CHAPTER III.

THE CAMPAIGN OF 1865.

Never, since the first gun was fired at Sumter, had the prospects of the Union cause appeared to be so nearly approximating a triumphant result, as at the commencement of the year 1865. While the rebels were daily, and almost hourly, losing all hope and confidence of success, while, one after another, their avenues of supplies and munitions of war were being closed to them, while their men, losing all faith in the promises of their leaders, were deserting daily by hundreds, and while their legislative assemblies were becoming disorderly, and disorganized meetings where personal abuse and mutual recriminations had long since taken the place of orderly and proper debate,—even the most faint-hearted of those who had the interests of the nation at heart, had begun to take courage, and to see the dawn of a brighter day at length approaching. Sherman had made his triumphant "march to the sea;" Fort Fisher had been captured and the Cape Fear River, one of the principal blockade running ports, had thus been effectually closed; Charleston was soon to fall and Sumter once more bore the old flag aloft.

The rebel press, though arrogant and blatant to the last, in its gross perversion of facts and its earnest endeavors to convert any disaster to the Union arms, however trifling, into a great Confederate victory, gave evident tokens, of a conviction, gradually growing in force and spreading far and wide through the South, that the frustration of their schemes was at hand, that secession was a failure and its days numbered. The Richmond *Whig*, Petersburg *Express*, and various other papers, tools of the rebel government, in a series of articles, plausibly and cleverly written and well calculated to deceive the unlettered masses of the South, claimed for the South a better condition, than they had known since the commencement of the war. Their army was reported by them to be well fed, clothed and sheltered, the spirits and courage of the men to be excellent and a certain and sure triumph of the Confederate cause, was prophecied as about to be the result of the commencement of hostilities, in which Lee would take the initiative in the spring.

On our side of the lines in front of Petersburg, however, a contrary impression prevailed, and as the winter wore away, even the most despondent began to cheer up as the hollowness of the Confederacy became apparent, the most obtuse could see that the beginning of the end was approaching, and all were looking forward to a speedy crushing out and final extinction of the last spark of rebellion.

Throughout the whole of the long dreary winter, night after night, shivering and half famished, miserably clothed, worse fed, and wretchedly armed, the rebel pickets had deserted their posts and came into our lines, all telling the same tale of suffering, deprivation and disaffection. Sometimes singly, sometimes in squads of three or four, or even greater numbers, they preferred running their chances of being shot, by our men or their own, to lingering on, suffering from cold and hunger, with an equal chance of being eventually either shot or hung. The Army of the Potomac, on the other hand, which had been comfortably hutted and furnished with the best of food and clothing, through the winter, had received a large accession to its numbers, both in recruits and also in convalescents from the different hospitals ; our leisure hours had been passed in resting from the severe campaign of the preceding year, with drilling enough to give us exercise, keep us in health, and to render us more efficient as soldiers. The numerous desertions from the rebels and the many successive Union victories had instilled confidence in the minds of our men, just in proportion as it had dispirited and demoralized the rebels, all felt sure of victory, and that the end was at hand.

The commencement of the year found the 37th in winter quarters on the Baxter road, just in front of their old battle field of the 17th of June, and in rear of Fort Morton. Considerable addition had been made to our numbers during the winter ; a large majority had had an opportunity of visiting their homes and friends ; our casualties had been few and the health and spirits of the entire regiment were excellent. With increasing satisfaction, as each day's mail brought tidings of further Union successes, we watched the net closing tighter and closer around rebeldom and began to look forward toward the prospect of a speedy return to our homes.

As the severer rigors of winter passed off, and the mild, warm days of an early spring began to awaken the vegetable world from its long sleep, the enemy, who had for some months, been remarkably quiet and civil, commenced annoying us by assailing us with mortar and Parrott shells whenever we attempted to indulge in a brigade drill or dress parade. These exhibitions of animosity, however, beyond driving a few timid natures to the doubtful security of pine trees and stumps, soon ceased to create much excitement and served mainly as an excellent preparation to accustom the ears of our new recruits to the sound of these missiles. Nobody ever got hurt by them, and nobody cared much for them. In the month of March we were visited by several severe tornadoes which threw down a number of the trees, among which our camp was built, and, on one occasion, killed one man, Corporal Kenneday of company F.

And so the time wore on, till at length an order came "one fine day" for all Sutlers to go to the base at City Point, for officers and men to turn in all their superfluous winter clothing, and for all arms and ammunition to be thoroughly inspected. The Army of the Potomac was stripping for the fight. Again a few days and rumors, undefined and indistinct at first, but gaining plausibility as time passed on, began to circulate through our camps that "Sheridan had come." And sure enough, one fine summer like spring morning, three or four wild, rough-looking individuals mounted on lean, but tough wiry animals, rode into our camp, clothed in Confederate uniform, and on being seized and questioned, declared themselves, not without a certain pride in so doing, to be " scouts in the service of General Sheridan " In confirmation, they pointed to a long line of dust, in rear of our camp, where, with the aid of our field glasses, we could dimly discern a large column of cavalry filing slowly along towards the left, in full view of the enemy and within range of his guns, proudly, defiantly, as if the mere fact of their being Sheridan's men, were a safeguard in itself.

This looked like business, and we prepared ourselves accordingly, remaining for the next three weeks in a continued state of excitement and expectation. On one occasion we thought the fun had commenced, a succession of loud cheers, or rather yells, accompanied by rapid and continued firing from the picket line on our left, leading us to suppose that Gen. Lee had opened the ball by taking the initiative himself, and was about to try the strength of our position. We were quickly under arms, and drawn up in line of battle, in the rear of Fort Morton, ready to move, wherever fate and the commanding general might choose to send us. Having waited there for an hour cr two, and the disturbance, which turned out to be nothing more than a mere picket *emeute*, having gradually quieted down, we were permitted to return in peace to our camp.

But more stirring scenes in the drama were at hand, time was rolling along, and the 25th of March and 2d of April were approaching. The rebellion, which the most sanguine of us never expected to end before July, was even then tottering to its fall, and a few weeks more were to see its final overthrow.

Ever since the nocturnal picket skirmish, I have mentioned above, the general commanding the division had impressed on us the necessity of exercising an extra amount of vigilance and caution; trench guards were doubled, the constant supervision of the picket line and reports as to the vigilance and efficiency of officers and men on duty there, were rendered an imperative part of the duties of the brigade officer of the day; brigade and regimental commanders exercised, in most cases, a sleepless and cat-like supervision of everything that occurred within the rebel lines, within their scope of observation; the signal man on the Avery House waved his flags and lanterns, frantically, day and night; our days were spent with field glasses and telescopes stuck to our eyes as if they grew there, and our night's rest was broken by orders sent round three or four times a night exacting the observance of the greatest vigilance or demanding information as to the movements of the enemy.

Our position became like that of "Sister Ann" in Bluebeard's tower and the part of Fatima, was, as the play bills say, "ably sustained" by our commanding generals, in their perpetual demands, as to whether "We saw anybody coming?"

On the morning of the 25th of March we were aroused from such restless sleep as we were in the habit of taking in those days, by the sound of three shots fired in rapid succession from the rebel lines, and quickly followed by a scattering fire of musketry A very few minutes sufficed for the donning of arms and accoutrements, and in less time than it takes to read this page, we were under arms and awaiting orders.

Meantime the batteries on either side had opened and were keeping up a very lively interchange of missiles; close on our right the second brigade was evidently warmly engaged, as a lively musketry fire, enlivened once in a while with the report of a heavy gun, testified The morning was dull and cloudy and nothing had yet occurred to enable us to form any conclusion as to what was on hand, but, after a few minutes we were ordered down to the right of the brigade and drawn up on the flank, at right angles to the main line of works, and here we began to gather an inkling of the facts of the case.

Right in our front, on an eminence on the opposite side of a ravine, on one side of which we lay snugly ensconsed behind a light line of works, was Fort Steadman, a large and very strong work built on Hare Hill, the spot where we had encamped nearly a year ago, just after the battle of the 18th of June. In and around this a fierce fight was going on, and to the rear of it were to be seen flashes, indicating that sharp skirmishing was going on in the direction of Meade Station. The truth was at once apparent. Massing his forces under cover of the night and taking advantage of the darkness of the morning and the close proximity of our lines, the enemy had driven in our picket line, surprised the garrison of the fort and captured it, and was now pushing for the City Point Railroad, and, perhaps, City Point itself, in fact *our lines were broken.*

By the time we had arrived at this conclusion, which was anything but a pleasant one, the firing in our rear had increased considerably, and daylight having at length fairly asserted its supremacy, we could see the rebel troops falling rapidly back into Fort Steadman. It had also become sufficiently light for our artillery to get the range and open on the fort, which they were now doing with a will, making their pieces speak with vigor and much to the purpose. This fact the rebels seemed fully to appreciate and regulated the duration of their second visit to the fort to a merely *passing* one, passing right through and over the parapet on the other side, back to their own lines as fast as possible. The cause of their retreat was soon apparent. Just as they commenced leaving, the third division of the 9th corps, under Brevet Major General Hartranft, appeared coming up over the edge of the ravine, advancing in line of battle in excellent order, and with the General at their head leading the charge. On they go, unbroken and unwavering, leaving here and there a man on the field, but never stopping or faltering. The "Johnnies" don't like the look of things, they evidently think they are in a tight place, "and have waked up the wrong passenger." And so they take their leave, *piling* over the parapets and swarming back to their lines like bees from a hive, leaving behind them hundreds of their dead and wounded, ten battle flags and any quantity of arms and accoutrements. A great number prefer taking their chances of a Union prison to facing Union bullets, and throwing away their arms, sneak in under cover of our breastworks and surrender themselves as prisoners of war. Meanwhile the 3d division has occupied Fort Steadman, the firing has ceased and the 37th goes home to breakfast, having for the first and only time been disengaged spectators of a battle.

The regiment suffered no loss in this affair, as although exposed to some shelling, it was not directly engaged with any portion of the enemy's forces, remaining on the field solely for the purpose of covering the right flank and rear of the 1st brigade.

The next week was passed in an uneasy, ominous state of comparative quiet, the lull that always precedes a storm of any kind whatever, broken by occasional rumors and reports, and sundry turnings out at unseasonable hours of the day and night. At length, on the evening of Saturday, the 1st of April, our chief, suspecting that Lee was about to evacuate, directed our batteries to feel the enemy's line, so as to find out, if possible, whether he had withdrawn his artillery or not. About half past ten the performance commenced, and the 37th was ordered to fall in, as usual, and move down to the support of our picket line.

Shortly after we had moved out of camp, the enemy began replying with his mortars, showing that these, at least, had not been removed, and, from their fire, one of our men was wounded as we marched down the new covered way leading to our picket line. We soon got into position in a deep valley or ravine, just in the rear of our picket line, and there, for about three hours, were witnesses of one of the most sublime and terrific spectacles of the war. Every gun and every mortar along the whole length of the two opposing lines was, by this time, fairly in action, and the various missiles, plainly to be traced in their course through the air, by the train of sparks from the burning fuse, were crossing one another at every angle and in every direction. Watching this grand pyrotechnic display from a secure and tolerably comfortable position, time passed rapidly enough, till about half past twelve, on the morning of Sunday, the 2d of April, when, the firing having gradually died away, we were ordered to march out by the left flank and report at Brigade Headquarters.

Arriving here, we were quickly joined by the 8th and 27th Michigan, 38th Wisconsin, and 109th New York, the 51st Pennsylvania, with a company from each of the other regiments, being left to take care of the picket line on our brigade front. After a short delay, we moved rapidly off towards the left, and about an hour before daylight were formed in line of battle in Fort Sedgwick, or, as it is better known, "Fort Hell," the business that brought us there being to support a charge that our 3d Division was about to make on Fort Mahone, otherwise known as "Fort Damnation."

These works bore the reputation of being the strongest and most formidable on the two lines, and it was with rather dubious feelings that we waited for the signal to advance, and the words of Brutus:

> —"Oh that a man might know
> The end of this day's business, e're it come!
> But it sufficeth, that the day will end,
> And the end is known."

occurred to many of us, probably more than once, through the course of the eventful day that was just beginning to dawn. At last the order is given, and silently and rapidly, just as the first grey streaks of dawn begin to shine in the east, we see the dusky forms file out past us into the open field beyond the fort. Then our turn comes next, and away we go with orders to keep as far to the left as we can get. On we go, grape, canister and case shot whistling round us in every direction, over a cornfield with the dried stalks still standing—over our picket line—across a small marshy run—"this must be the rebel picket line!" "hullo, there's a dead Johnny!" and in another minute we have retaliated on the rebels for their attrck of the 25th of March, and Fort Mahone and two or three hundred yards of the rebel works are in possession of the 1st Brigade, 1st Division of the 9th Army Corps.

At daylight, we discover that during the darkness and confusion, two companies of our regiment have separated somewhat from the rest, and are lying in Fort Mahone, while the remainder of the regiment lie a little to the right of that work. We hold our position all through that day, while fighting is going on on each side of us, from the Appomattox to the extreme left, and away round to the Five-forks, where Wright and Sheridan are busy at work. But we have no time to think of what is going on, on either side of us, events in our own neighborhood demand all our attention. Several times, in the course of the day, the rebels attempt to regain the fort, and as often we send them back till the hillside in our front is thick with dead and dying.

And so the 2d of April draws to a close, the rebel line is broken and the city of Petersburg is, virtually, ours. All that night we pass, under arms, in the rebel works, and at daylight on the 3d, advance in line of battle, not a shot from the enemy to check our progress—we can see the cannon remaining in several of the forts, but where are the gunners?

> "Did traitors lurk in the *rebel* hold?
> Had their hands grown stiff or their hearts grown cold?
> I know not in sooth, but from yonder wall
> There flashed no fire, there hissed no ball."
> —*Siege of Corinth.*

and now we are up to the second line of works, they are silent and empty, and Gen. Hartranft, commanding the 3d Division of our Corps, jumps astride of the 8-inch Columbiad, which, a week or two before, had shelled his headquarters in the Avery House, and which he had sworn he would "straddle."

And now the fact becomes evident, *Petersburg is evacuated.* We break from line of battle into column, and dipping down into a ravine we see, as we mount the hill on the other side, the cockade city lying stretched out at our feet, the goal we have been striving for, for almost a year, is won, and Petersburg is ours.

It seems strange and dream-like, at first, to stand there and look down, at close quarters, on the spires and cupolas that for many a long month we have watched from a distance, and to trace their connections, with the buildings of which they formed a part, in reality, instead of only in imagination, as before.

Yes, there it lay before us looking, somehow, strangely civilized and peaceful with its old fashioned steep-roofed houses nestled down amongst the trees, the smoke from the chimneys curling upwards into the bright blue sky overhead—a crowd of darkies "Hurrahing and Hallelujahing" around us, accompanying their expressions of delight with a grotesque exhibition of antics and grimaces, and "*Bressing* de Lord and the Yankees," about alike, for the freedom that had this day come to them. And now as the light gets stronger, we see the colors of the 2d Michigan waving from the Court House, and the strains of a brass band come floating down the wind faint and indistinct in the distance. But a note here and there is sufficient to show that it is a salute to the flag that waves over the captured city, and, as the well-known strains of the "Star Spangled Banner" fall clearer and clearer on the ear, our own flags are "unfurled to the glad breeze of heaven," and a cheer goes up to greet them, that awakens the echoes of the city far and wide.

We sit down under the shade of the locust trees and

discuss a hasty breakfast, when the word is given, "Fall in," and we march back to camp, to bid farewell to the spot that, for nearly six months, has been our only home, to pack up our Lares and Penates and transporting them, like Ulysses, (not Grant, but him of Troy) on our back, start off in pursuit of the rebel army, or wherever it may please Grant to send us.

The same evening the brigade was moved out on to the Boydton Plankroad where the men were allowed a brief rest after a week of duty, which had pretty well tired us all out, both officers and men. It is true that we had had little or no marching, and only one day's fighting, but the continual state of tension in which our nerves were kept all that time, and the want of rest, made us all glad of a respite from our labors.

We remained camped near the city till the 6th of the month, Col. Ely, commanding 2d brigade, 1st division, 9th army corps, being appointed Military Governor of the same, Brevet Major General Wilcox, commanding the district. We found the inhabitants, for the most part, orderly and well disposed, though a few cases of outrage towards our troops occurred which were as much deprecated and resented by the more orderly and well behaved portion of the community, as by us.

PETERSBURG is a remarkably neat and pretty city, situated on the Appmatox River, about ten miles above its confluence with the James at City Point. Before the war it contained somewhere in the neighborhood of twenty thousand inhabitants, though at the time of our occupation of it, its population scarcely numbered over fifteen thousand. It was originally a trading post, established by one Peters, for traffic with the Indians, and in process of time, and as the country became settled, became a place of trade for the settlers in the vicinity. The original town was located about where the cemetery at Blandford now stands, and for a time, was known as Peter's, afterwards as Pocahontas, this latter name being still given to a hamlet across the river, forming a suburb of the city. The name was finally changed to Petersburg which it retains to this day; it is situated principally in Dinwiddie county, and is the principal tobacco shipping point in the South. The neighboring counties of Prince George and Pocahontas, have a fertile, highly productive soil, raising corn, tobacco, sugar-cane and cotton as well as wheat, barley, oats and other cereals. It has railroad communications with Richmond, distant twenty-five miles, Burkesville sixty miles, Weldon, N. C., seventy-five miles, Norfolk and Suffolk sixty-three miles, and a short railroad also connects it with City Point, its port of entry, to which place there is easy access, from the coast, for vessels drawing fifteen feet of water.

There are several large cotton, flour, and lumber mills erected on the rapids of the Appomattox, which furnish an unequalled water power, as yet only partially developed, and a proper attention paid to which would largely increase the wealth and importance of the place. The streets are wide and straight, nicely ornamented with shade trees, and the public buildings, for the most part, well designed and well finished. In hotels the city is rather deficient, there being but one decent one, the Jarrett House, in the whole place. Sycamore street, the principal business street of the city, contains a few fine buildings and stores, and quite a number of handsome residences.

The stores were mostly closed on our arrival, and but few of them had much of a stock on hand, Confederate scrip having for a long time been quoted "low" and the supply scant. On the Saturday preceding the Monday on which we arrived in the city, flour had been sold at $1,400 a barrel, wood $50 a cord and other necessaries of life in proportion. The lower part of the city bore severe traces of the siege, hardly a house being unmarked by either shot or shell. The gas works were nearly torn to pieces, a long chimney, eighty-five feet in height, which had once formed part of the building, having been thrown down a short time before our arrival, after having received thirty-five shells through it in different places. The clock on the Town Hall had also been perforated by a three inch shell, though strange to say, the missile had not damaged the works in the least. Two bridges across the Appomattox and three large warehouses full of tobacco, had been set on fire and destroyed by the rebels when they evacuated. A fine strong bridge leading across the river, from the South Side railroad depot to the railway company's machine shop, had been loaded with two new locomotives and all the cars that could be placed on it, and then set fire to, cars and locomotives being thus precipitated into the river.

A large quantity of commissary stores, consisting of corn meal, bacon, coffee, (unroasted,) sugar and tobacco, was found in the rebel government warehouses and were afterwards issued to the destitute citizens, irrespective of color. Captain John Cooper, of the 5th Wisconsin, was appointed C. S., and the scene in his office, from daylight till dark, was a novel one.

Ladies of the first family type, clothed in deepest black, with a sullen, defiant look on their handsome faces, sometimes closely veiled; Africa, of all shades, from the genuine sable "mungo," with skin like polished ebony, and showing from between his extended gums a formidable array of ivory, to the graceful quadroon, hardly a shade darker, and very often a great deal handsomer than her late mistress, standing within a few feet of one another, all jubilant and triumphant, all rejoicing in their new found freedom, kind and polite to the boys in blue, their liberators, and obsequious, to a degree, to shoulder straps. Poor things, what their future may be, we know not, but they can never know a happier day in their lives, than when, there on the third of April, 1865, the fetters fell from their hands, as from Paul and Silas in prison, and they stood, for the first time in their lives, free men and women.

On the 6th of April, the 1st division, 9th army corps, was relieved from duty in Petersburg, and moved out on the line of the South Side Railroad, having its headquarters at Burkesville, and the corps being strung along the road from that place to Petersburg. The 37th moved out at daylight and camped about dark near Ford's Station, from whence they were afterwards removed to beyond Wellsville and in the neighborhood of Black's and White's, where they remained till after the surrender of Lee and Johnston and their armies, guarding the railroad and the farms and plantations adjoining, and administering, as far as our commissariat would permit, to the wants of the adjacent population.

Overrun and devastated by two contending armies, the once rich country, surrounding Petersburg and Richmond, is to-day a wilderness. Not only have the crops been swept off to supply the wants of the Confederate soldiers, but the cattle and horses have been also absorbed for the same purpose. Fences have been torn down and burnt, houses, sheds and barns stripped of their coverings to furnish huts for winter quarters, and the whole country converted into a scene of devastation and ruin. Deserters from both armies have formed bands of guerrillas for the purposes of plunder and pillage, men from the opposing armies having in some cases associated together for this purpose.

A rather amusing incident of this kind which occurred whilst we were near Black's and White's, may serve as an illustration. Col. Harriman, having been informed that large body of guerrillas had formed a camp in his neighborhood, sent Capt. Burnett, A. D. C. on his staff, accompanied by a sufficient force, to reconnoitre and report on the condition of affairs. The Captain set out on his expedition and soon arrived in sight of the enemy, (?)

whom he found to consist of about a couple of hundred colored individuals camped in due form, and with camp guards, &c., duly posted. The *commanding officer* was a private of the 5th Mass. Colored Cavalry, who had, by some means or other, strayed from his command, and had, like David, "gathered to him every one (of his color) that was in distress and every one that was discontented," and had established a camp in regular military style.

The sable chieftain sat at his tent door as the Captain approached, and while one intelligent son of Africa was carefully cleaning his master's (?) horse, another highly intellectual contraband was blacking his boots. The scene was a rich one and might be taken for the frontispiece of Mrs Harriet Beecher Stowe's next novel. The terms of capitulation were not, we believe, quite as ceremonious nor so advantageous as those agreed on between Gens. Grant and Lee, for poor Cuffee was sent back to his regiment under arrest, and his sable warriors who belonged to the neighboring plantations. dispersed to their homes, and their arms, which they had collected from the battle field of the Five Forks, turned over to Uncle Sam.

Whilst camped here the sad news reached us of the brutal assassination of President Lincoln by the wretched maniac, Booth, and I say maniac, not to palliate his crime, but because his act was one none but a maniac would have committed. For, however much he may have sympathized with the Southern cause and hated its fancied oppressors, he might have known that such an expression of malignity and revenge, even though sanctioned by the Confederate government, as after events have shown it was, would, as it in fact has, crush out all sympathy for the rebellion, at home and abroad, and extinguish the last sentiment of pity for what its partisans have been pleased to call their heroic resistance against superior numbers.

The effect the news of the assassination had on the army may be imagined, but cannot be described. In the midst of our rejoicings at the successes which had so lately crowned our efforts, and while the praises and acclamations of the North were yet ringing in our ears, it fell on us like a thunderbolt. Just as the dawn of peace, crowning the long and arduous labors of the past four years, was beginning to illuminate his pathway, in the very zenith of his career and at the heighth of his fame, our good, kind President was ruthlessly and brutally murdered. There is no need here to eulogize those virtues, so well known to all who have watched so anxiously and with such interest the successive acts of his career, nor to enlarge on that stubborn honesty and integrity of purpose and principle which has brought this nation safely through a sea of troubles which well nigh overwhelmed it. Abraham Lincoln has gone to his account, and the tears of a nation that honored him whilst living, follow him to the grave, now that he is dead. The loss is ours, not his; he has died at his post with his harness on his back; he has laid down his life for the country he loved more than life itself, a soldier in the cause of humanity, freedom and right, and what could man wish more. Peace to his soul! When the time comes for us to go, may our record, if not as glorious, be at least as clear as his.

REUNION.

[*From the London Spectator.*]

An end at last! The echoes of the war—
   The weary war beyond the western waves—
Die in the distance. Freedom's rising star
   Beacons above a hundred thousand graves:

The graves of heroes who have won the fight,
   Who in the storming of the stubborn town
Have rung the marriage peal of might and right,
   And scaled the cliffs and cast the dragon down.

Pæans of armies thrill across the sea,
   Till Europe answers—"Let the struggle cease,
The bloody page is turned; the next may be
   For ways of pleasantness and paths of peace!—

A golden morn—a dawn of better things—
   The olive-branch—clasping of hands again—
A noble lesson read to conquering kings—
   A sky that tempests had not scoured in vain.

This from America we hoped and him
   Who ruled her "in the spirit of his creed."
Does the hope last when all our eyes are dim,
   As History records her darkest deed?

The pilot of his people through the strife,
   With his strong purpose turning scorn to praise,
E'en at the close of battle reft of life,
   And fair inheritance of quiet days.

Defeat and triumph found him calm and just,
   He showed how clemency should temper power,
And dying left to future times in trust
   The memory of his brief victorious hour.

O'ermastered by the irony of fate,
   The last and greatest martyr of his cause;
Slain like Achilles at the Scæan gate,
   He saw the end, and fixed "the purer laws."

May these endure and, as his work, attest
   The glory of his honest heart and hand—
The simplest, and the bravest, and the best—
   The Moses and the Cromwell of his land.

> Too late the pioneers of modern spite,
>   Awe-stricken by the universal gloom.
> See his name lustrous in Death's sable night,
>   And offer tardy tribute at his tomb.
>
> But we who have been with him all the while,
>   Who knew his worth, and loved him long ago,
> Rejoice that in the circuit of our isle
>   There is no room at last for Lincoln's foe."

The surrender of Lee and Johnston with their entire armies, put an end to the rebellion in Virginia, and left the Army of the Potomac, for the first time in four years, out of employment, with no one to fight and looking round for some one to hit or to "tread on the tail of its coat." Such things could not last, so on the 20th of April we had orders to pack up and move from our camp on the South Side railroad to City Point, there to take transports for Washington. This we accordingly did, and after a tiresome march, arrived at City Point on the morning of the 22d.

A few hours sufficed for all necessary arrangements, and before evening the steamer *Daniel Webster*, having on board Col. Harriman and staff, Gen. Humphries of the 2d corps, and the 37th and 38th Wisconsin, was steaming slowly down the James river against a strong flood tide. We passed Harrison's Landing, where the 9th corps crossed the James on pontoons in its march from Cold Harbor to Petersburg, during the summer of last year, and just below this point, the last rays of the setting sun were shining on the glorious old stars and stripes floating proudly over Fort Powhattan, the strongest work on the James river. Our boat having no regular government pilot, was compelled to anchor shortly after dark, and wait till morning and daylight should enable us to pick our way along the miny channel. We passed Fortress Monroe with its "even trench" and frowning embrasures about sunrise, and steamed out through Hampton Roads, past that singularly amphibious locality, part fort, part prison, known as the Rip Raps, into the smooth waters of Chesapeake Bay. The morning was still and pleasant, a light breeze from the northwest created just enough swell to give an easy rise and fall to the vessel, enough to make us feel that we were at sea, and hardly enough to unsettle the internal arrangements of the least nautical of our passengers. Far away on the starboard bow, Capes Charles and Henry were just visible, faint blue streaks in the distant offing. Astern of us were Norfolk, Fortress Monroe, the Rip Raps, several Men of War, including two British and one French steam frigate, and several saucy looking Yankee gunboats, bustling round in a great hurry, making a great swell in the water and a great noise with their escaping steam, as if they had important government business on hand and were anxious to get through with it. Schooners, barques and sloops of all sizes, builds and styles were either dropping easily down before the light wind, their big fore-and-aft sails boomed out on either side and giving them the appearance, as they rose and fell on the swells, of sea-birds, perched on the water, with their wings spread ready to take flight, or with sheets flat aft were working up the bay, passing and repassing one another as they tacked and tacked again. And the huge steam frigates lay there quiet, and, as it seemed, disdainful watchers of the whole scene, models of order and neatness from truck to deck, every rope taut and in its place, each spar and every line clear and distinct against the blue sky behind them, the black muzzles of the guns with their white tompions all in even line, and the boats at the swinging boom, each with its boat-tender aboard to keep it from chafing and rubbing against its neighbor—everything orderly, methodical, neat. (And here a moral. What a pity some people in this world cannot, like a man-of-war's boat, be furnished with a boat-tender, to keep the waves of envy and unfriendliness from causing them to chafe against their fellows.)

But ethics and moralizing have but little to do with the 1st brigade, 1st division, 9th army corps, and still less with the good ship *Daniel Webster*, which, about this time, was bowling along up the bay, at the rate of ten knots an hour. About noon we passed the light-ship on Wolf Trap Shoals, with the *tin-clad* lying alongside, to protect her from guerrillas. For, the inference being but fair that those fiends, who would not hesitate to destroy a train containing innocent women and children, would have as little compunction in destroying the oftentimes only friend of the storm-beaten ship, in her most thrilling hours of danger, all the light-houses and light-vessels along the coast of Virginia are strongly guarded, day and night. Just before dark, we entered the mouth of the Potomac, and, in obedience to a hail from the guard-ship, at Port Washington, made fast to the dock at Alexandria, at sunrise, on the morning of the 24th. Here we disembarked, and were marched out to a very pleasant camping-ground, on the line of the Orange and Alexandria railroad. We remained here two days, when we received orders to march to Washington. Thither we accordingly went, and the evening of the same day found us encamped near Tenallytown, between Forts Gaines and Simmons, and not far from the Chain Bridge. Here we remained, "possessing our souls in peace," and doing a little picket duty, a little drilling, not a little dress-parading. and, in fact, playing soldiers; with nothing to do, and all day to do it in; and, barring a slight suspicion of monotony, leading a not unpleasant life.

On Tuesday evening, May 9th, we had a very pleasant reunion, at brigade headquarters, the occasion being the presentation to Col. Harriman, by the officers of his staff, of a very handsome sword. The presentation was made, in the name of the staff, by Capt. Charles McCreery, 8th Michigan Volunteers, Inspector General, who in a very neat and appropriate speech descanted on the pleasant nature of the relations that had always existed between the Colonel and his staff, officially and otherwise, during the long time he had commanded the brigade, and speaking in terms of the warmest commendation of the able and efficient manner in which the Colonel had commanded the brigade both in camp and in action. The Colonel responded, briefly and to the purpose, and after an hour or so spent in social chat the party broke up, pleased and gratified at the opportunity that had been afforded them of showing their appreciation of an able and gallant officer.

When the last grand pageant of the war passed through the streets of the capital, and the army, that for the last four years, had been laboring to maintain the existence of the country and to uphold its chosen form of government, received a sincere and hearty public welcome at the hands of a grateful people. Our regiment took a part in the pageant and received its share of the welcome. For two days, Washington was the scene of a military display, the like of which the world has never seen, and God grant may never have occasion to see again. From nine in the morning till three in the afternoon of each day, Pennsylvania Avenue, from the Capitol to Georgetown, was covered with troops, as the armies of the Potomac, Tennessee and Georgia passed along through crowds of their fellow citizens who had turned out to welcome them home.

The long wide street, with its shady sidewalks and handsome buildings, was dressed in its gayest. The fresh spring verdure of the trees, the glorious stripes and stars waving everywhere, the bright glancing bayonets, set off by the dark blue of their bearers, the regimental colors and guidons, the waving of flags and handkerchiefs from every window, the lively strains of the various brigade and regimental bands, the bright clear sky and sun overhead, formed a sight once seen, never to be forgotten, and worth ten years of a man's life for him to be able to say, "I was there."

But the details of this brilliant military panorama are now history, so suffice it to say that the 37th contributed their part to the show and received their welcome from the Washingtonians and their friends.

On the afternoon of the 25th of May, the 1st brigade was reviewed by Colonel Harriman and a large party of distinguished visitors, guests of Colonel H's. The party included Governor Lewis, Gen. Lucius Fairchild, Gen. Gaylord, Brev. Brig. Gen. C. Fairchild, Governor Crapo of Michigan, Major Chas. Hamlin, son of the late Vice President, and his sister, Mrs. Bachelor, Col. Proudfit of Wisconsin, Mrs. Gen. Fairchild, and a large delegation of civilians and soldiers from Michigan and Wisconsin.

The review was preceded by brigade dress parade, followed by a short drill, after which the ranks were opened and Col. Harriman, accompanied by the two Governors, Gens. Fairchild and Gaylord, rode along the front and rear of the line, the ranks were then closed and the brigade, having formed column by company, marched past in review. Great praise was awarded for the accuracy and regularity with which the whole affair passed off, by all present, both civil and military.

At our camp in Tenallytown we remained without any occurrence of moment coming to break the monotony of our lives, daily expecting an order to return home, and daily being disappointed.

The orders mustering out all men sick in hospital and all whose term of service expired before October 1st, 1865, reduced us much in number, and an effort was made to consolidate the 38th with us.

In the early part of July an order, directing the consolidation to take place, was received, but was again countermanded, in consequence of an order from the War Department to muster out the whole 9th corps.

Some reason or the other, no doubt a good and sufficient one, delayed the order, however, for some time on its passage from the Adjutant General's office in Washington, causing no little grumbling and a great many *curse*-ory remarks from our men. It came at length, and on the morning of July 26th, at 10 A. M., the 37th Wisconsin, after having served for nearly half its original term of enlistment, and having spent most of that time in active and arduous campaigning, ceased to belong to the service of the United States. The same evening, transportation having been duly furnished us, we took the cars on the Baltimore and Ohio railroad for Baltimore. A detachment of the 38th Wisconsin and the 27th Michigan occupied the same train as we did, and as we rolled out of the depot a cheer went up from the forty-three cars, of which our train was composed, that wakened the echoes far and near.

From Baltimore we took the Pennsylvania railroad for Pittsburg, where the Ladies' Aid Society gave us a most hospitable reception. From Pittsburg, through the winding glens of Pennsylvania, and over the teeming fields of Ohio, till at length, tired, dusty, and hungry, at two o'clock in the morning we sweep into the evergreen city of Cleveland.

Here too, the ladies, God bless them, are on hand with a first rate breakfast ready and waiting for us. After a short delay we embarked on board the *Morning Star*, and made a quick and pleasant run across Lake Erie and through the St. Clair river, till at length we cited the old fashioned looking buildings of Sandwich and Windsor, looking sleepily and wonderingly at the bustling, lively aspect of their opposite neighbor, Detroit.

Here we came in for a share of the kind and hearty welcome that awaited the 27th Michigan, and here we took leave of that regiment. For over a year we had served in the same brigade; for over a year the 37th " Badgers " and 27th " Wolverines " had toiled, marched and fought side by side. And it was with mutual feelings of esteem and regret that in the streets of Detroit we parted with our old companions in arms. Many a hearty good-bye and God speed you were exchanged and many promises of correspondence given and received, and soon the cars whirled us on, through the night, to where the ladies of Grand Haven had a good breakfast ready for us, where they greeted us with a hearty welcome,

"and hands that offer fruit and flowers,"

There too, was McBride, prince of Captains, and the famous old *Detroit*, and with such favorable conjunction of boat and captain, our run across the lake was safely and expeditiously accomplished.

A hearty welcome met us at the City of Bricks, and our greeting, on our return to our State, was all that could be desired. We arrived at Madison about 4 o'clock in the afternoon of Monday, July 31st, were entertained at the Railroad Depot at the expense of the State, and were welcomed in the park around the Capitol by the Governor, Secretary of State, Adjutant General and the Municipal authorities of Madison. The Regiment was then furloughed for fifteen days with orders to report, at the expiration of that time, at Camp Randall.

And here we will leave them at the point from which they started, welcomed back to a country jubilant and exultant in a peace they themselves had helped to win, rejoicing themselves in the prospect of seeing home and friends once more.

And even as now, when their warfare is accomplished and the victory won, we gladly sheath the sword and lay aside the musket, so if the old Badger State ever again calls on her sons to stand forth in her defence, none will respond more readily than the

THIRTY-SEVENTH WISCONSIN INFANTRY.

TABLE

SHOWING GAIN AND LOSS

OF

Thirty-Seventh Wisconsin Volunteers

DURING CAMPAIGNS OF 1864 AND 1865.

COMPANY.

	A	B	C	D	E	F	G	H	I	K	
Original strength	83	83	83	83	82	80	83	81	80	80	818
Recruits { 1864	1	...	1	7	5	5	...	2	...	...	21
{ 1865	9	...	2	5	8	8	11	6	7	7	63
Draft { 1863	...	...	1	...	...	...	...	...	...	...	1
{ 1864	13	18	15	17	14	7	16	21	8	8	137
Substitutes	3	8	3	1	4	4	8	...	16	10	57
Total	109	109	106	113	113	104	118	110	111	106	1097

LOSS.

	A	B	C	D	E	F	G	H	I	K	
By death	18	22	18	20	27	28	24	21	16	22	216
By discharge	6	6	13	11	10	19	4	12	24	10	115
By transfer to V. R. C.	...	3	...	4	3	2	2	4	...	1	19
By desertion	4	2	1	0	1	0	5	2	7	6	28
Total	28	33	32	*38	41	49	35	39	47	39	378

COMMISSIONED OFFICERS—FIELD AND STAFF.

	A	B	C	D	E	F	G	H	I	K	
Original strength	3	3	3	3	3	3	3	3	3	9	
Killed and died of wounds	1	1	1	1	1	...	...	...	2	...	7
Died of disease	1	...	...	1	...	...	...	...	...	...	2
Resigned	...	...	1	...	1	...	...	1	...	1	3	7
Discharged	...	1	1	...	1	...	2	1	...	...	6
Dismissed	...	...	...	...	...	...	...	...	1	...	1
Mustered out	...	...	...	...	...	...	...	...	1	...	2	3
Total loss	2	2	3	2	3	...	2	2	3	5	26

* Including three men transferred to the 38th Wis. Vol. Inf.

ORIGINAL ROSTER
OF FIELD, STAFF AND LINE OFFICERS
37TH WISCONSIN VOL. INF'TRY.

COLONEL.
SAM. HARRIMAN.
Promoted Brevet Brig. Gen., July 1865.

LIEUT. COLONEL.
ANSON. O. DOOLITTLE.
Resigned Sept. 7th, 1864.

MAJOR.
WM. J. KERSHAW.
Promoted Lieut. Col. Sept. 27, 1864; resigned Oct. 18, 1864.

ADJUTANT.
CLARON I. MILTIMORE.
Promoted Brevet Captain, July, 1865.

QUARTERMASTER.
WM. C. WEBB.
Promoted to Colonel 52d Wis. Vols.

SURGEON.
D. C. ROUNDY.

FIRST ASST. SURGEON.
GEORGE H. CALKINS.
Mustered out March 11th, 1864.

SECOND ASST. SURGEON.
JOHN HENRY ORRICK.
Promoted 1st Asst., March 11th, 1864.

CHAPLAIN.
LEWIS M. HAWES.
Resigned March 1865.

NON-COMMISSIONED STAFF.

Principal Musician—W. H. BURTON.
Commissary Sergeant—N. G. ROWLEY. Prom. 2d Lieut. Co. Dec. 29, 1864.
Quartermaster Sergeant—N. B. PRENTISS. Prom. Regimental Q. M.
Hospital Steward—PORTER M. ROUNDY.
Sergeant Major—GEO. GRAHAM. Prom. 1st Lt. Co. G, Dec. 29, 1864.

MUSTER ROLL OF "A" COMPANY.

Raised in Wood, Juneau, and Dane counties, by SAM. STEVENS and S. JONES. Mustered into U. S. service at Madison, Wisconsin, April 16th, 1864.

Captain.

SAMUEL STEVENS. Killed in action, June 18th, 1864.

First Lieutenant.

SANFORD JONES. Died in hospital, Aug. 18th, 1864; promoted Captain, July 18th, 1864.

Second Lieutenant.

DANIEL A. LOWBER. Wounded, June 18th, 1864; promoted 1st Lieut., July 28th, Captain, Sept. 27th, 1864.

Sergeants.

Theo. M. Hobby, promoted 2d Lieut., July 18th; discharged, Dec. 22d, 1863.
Oliver H. Hunt, died in hospital, Dec. 16th, 1864.
Francis A. Barnard, wounded in action, June 18th, 1864, and discharged, March 8th, 1865.
Wm. Cobban, wounded in action, July 30th, and discharged, January 2d, 1865.
Ferdinand Herber, reduced to ranks, July 15th; wounded in action, July 30th, 1864.

Corporals.

Nelson H. Carney, reduced to ranks, July 1st, 1864.
Irvine J. Slattery, wounded in action, June 18th; promoted Sergt., Jan. 1st, 1865.
Edw. Z. Weed.
Tim. E. Wade, died in hospital, Nov. 7th, 1864.
Benj. F. Wheeler, killed in action, June 18th, 1864.
Jesse B. Hake.
Willis B. Moffatt.
Frank Wilson, wounded in action, June 18th, 1864.

Musicians.

Thoph. L. Hacker.
Calvin D. Rogers.

Privates.

Aldrich, Samuel K.
Alger, Joseph, promoted corporal, Jan. 1st, 1865.
Alger, Westley, taken prisoner in the crater, July 30th, 1864.
Allen, Thomas J., deserted in Baltimore, Md., May 1st, 1864.
Allen, Lewis, promoted Serg't, July 1st, 1864.
Anderson, Benjamin.
Angel, Byron A.
Arne, Courtland Z.
Black, William Jas., died, July 12th, 1864, of wounds received in action, June 18th, 1864.
Briggs, Thomas.
Carney, John, taken prisoner, July 30th, 1864, in the crater.
Carney, Nelson H.
Carter, Michael.
Collins, Cassious M.
Cooledge, George W., discharged for disability, Feb. 12th, 1864.
Cooley, Charles F.
Chartier, Narcisse, wounded in action, June 18th, 1864.
Davis, John, wounded in action, June 18th, 1864.
Davis, David, taken prisoner in action, April 2d, 1865.
Dodge, William H., transferred to company F, May 30th, 1864, for promotion.
Gamble, David, transferred to company F, June 10th, 1864.
Granger, Oliver.
Greenhalgh, John E., killed June 18th, 1864, near Petersburg, Va.
Goodbout, Charles, transferred from company F, May 30th, 1864.
Hasson, William, transferred to accept promotion, May 20th, 1864.
Hartman, John, wounded in action, June 18th, 1864; discharged for disability, June 1st, 1865.
Hawes, Chancey, B., promoted corporal, July 1st, 1864, and sergeant, Jan. 1st, 1865.
Hutchinson, Albert M.
Hurlburt, A. B. C., promoted corporal, March 1st, 1865.
Hutchinson, Robert.
Kelley, Thomas, deserted, March 18th, 1865.
Kimberly, Benjamin A.
Kenney, Thomas.
Lane, Jesse, died of wounds, July 7th, 1864.
Mills, Benjamin B.
Mountfort, John, deserted, Dec. 9th, 1864.
Morris, George P.
Moore, William H., promoted corporal, Dec. 7th, 1864.
Moses, Leonard H.

McCarty, William, deserted at Madison, Wisconsin, April 2? 1864.
McGunell, Michael, wounded in action, July 30th, 1864.
Odell, John A., discharged Oct. 15th, 1864.
Olson, Anum, died in hospital, Sept. 19th, 1864.
Paye, Martin.
Peterson, Peter, taken prisoner, July 30th, 1864, in the crater.
Peak, John, died of wounds, July 7th, 1864.
Plunewell, Henry, discharged, March 25th, 1865.
Ramsey, William.
Rensimer, Joseph, in action, June 17th, 1864; promoted corpor March 1st, 1865.
Riner, John, died in hospital, Nov. 14th, 1864.
Rood, Jas. B., promoted corporal, Dec. 7th, 1864.
Rosencrans, Anson C.
Sanders, Joel.
Sanford, Muuson B., killed in action, June 18th, 2864.
Scott, Walter, killed on picket, June 24th, 1864.
Scott, Corwin D., wounded, June 18th, 1864; discharged.
Slater, Charles G.
Smith, Josiah B., wounded in action, June 18th, 1864.
Smith, Robert N., wounded in action, July 30th, 1864.
Smith, William B., killed in action, June 18th, 1864.
Springer, Samuel, wounded in action, June 18th, 1864; died wounds, Sept. 4th, 1864.
Solles, Edgar.
Sterling, Wm., promoted corporal, Aug. 30th, 1864.
Thatcher, Thomas J., taken prisoner, July 30th, 1864; exchang' March 7th, 1865.
Tritt, Zenas C., promoted corporal, Jan. 1st, and sergeant, Mai 8th, 2865; wounded, July 30th, 1864.
Van Deustan, Edward N., killed in action, July 30th, 1864.
Waldo, Joseph.
Warner, James L, killed in action, June 18th, 1864.
Whitney, Almond, killed in action, June 28th, 1864.

RECRUITS, COMPANY A.

Volunteers.

James Gillin, wounded in action, April 2d, 1865.
Oramel E. Tupper.
Luther Fuller.
John McIntyre.
Jas. M. Plott.
Taylor Stevens.

Wm. Fuller.
Thos. Caley.
George Cline.
George Cox.

Drafted Mem.

Gideon Ardoss.
Leroy Beecher.
Adam Clawson.
Nich. Chambers.
Peter Gavin.
Reuben Gardner.
Owen Hillman.
B. H. W. Z. Kussow.
S. P. O'Neil.
Geo. W. Teal, promoted orderly sergeant, Dec. 22, 1864; and 1st Lieut., July 21st, 1865.
P Vanderlivoff.
John Wart.
Col. Wells.

Substitutes.

Charles White.
H. R. Clark.
F. N. Brasher.

MUSTER ROLL OF "B" COMPANY.

Raised in Oshkosh and Janesville by R. C. EDEN and WM. H. EARL. Mustered into U. S. service at Madison, Wis., by Capt. T. T. BRAND, U. S. A., April 13, 1864.

Captain.

R. C. EDEN. Promoted Major, Dec. 15th, 1864. Lieut. Col., July 21st, 1865. Brev. Lieut. Col. U. S. V.

First Lieutenant.

W. H. EARL. Died in Hospital, Washington, D. C., of wounds received in action, June 17th, 1864.

Second Lieutenant.

N. S. DAVISON. Wounded, June 18th, 1864. Promoted First Lieutenant, July 28th, 1864. Wounded Dec. 15th, 1864. Promoted Captain, Dec. 15th, 1864. Discharged for disability, ——— 1865.

Musicians.

Wm. Burton, appointed principal musician, July, 1864.
William Mason, transferred to Veteran Reserve Corps.

Sergeants.

L. D. Harmon, wounded June 17th; promoted 2d Lieut. July 23d, 1864; 1st Lieut , Dec. 15th, 1864; Captain, May, 1865.
J. E. Williamson, wounded Aug. 19th, 1884; promoted 2d Lieut., Dec. 15th, 1864; 1st Lieut., May, 1865.
T. D. Powers, wounded June 18th, 1864.
O. E. Rice, died Aug. 14th, of wounds received in action, July 30th, 1864.
Thos. A. Lockhart, wounded June 17th, 1864.

Corporals.

J. P. Braynard, transferred to field hospital.
E. S. Casler.
W. A. Barber.
E. Wheeler, wounded Suly 30th, 1864.
M. Lockerby, June 17th, 1864 ; transferred to Vet. Res. Corps.
Hy. G. Brown, died Aug. 3d of wounds received in action, June 17th, 1864.

Privates.

Allbee, Perry, transferred to Vet. Res. Corps.
Allen, W. S., promoted Sergeant.
Allen, Norman.
Babcock, Louis G.
Barnes, Wm. E., died at Depot Hospital, City Point, Nov. 10th, 1864.
Barnes, Hollis J., died at White Hall Hospital, Bucks county, Pa., January 17th, 1865.
Booth, Charles H., wounded June 17th, 1864.
Boyd, Robert M.
Boynton, Horace S., ambulance driver, 1st Div., 9th A. C. Train.
Cross, Otis, missing in action, July 30th, 1864.
Daikens, Amos.
Daikens, Ezra.
Denure, Jerome, wounded June 18th, 1864.
Devine, James B.
Doty, Isaiah.
Dunn, Charles.
Duley, John W., died in the State of disease—date unknown.
Dutcher, Horace.
Eaton, Cyrus R., died in hospital, Alexandria, Va.; date unknown.
Finley, Hugh, killed in action, June 18th, 1864.
France, Aquila.
Fuller, Napoleon, killed in trenches before Petersburg, July 6th, 1864.
Hall, John, killed in action June 17th, 1864.
Hinckley, Edward.
Holton, John C., died in post-hospital, Madison, Wis., Apr. 27th, 1864.
Howard, Abram.
Ingrahan, Eleazer S., wounded in action June 17th, 1864.
Laib, William C.
Lattin, Sylvester.
Lawrenz, John, wounded in action July 30th; left leg amputated.
Lee, Hugh, died in Armory Square Hospital, Washington, June 21st, 1864.
Luhm, Fred, died in Armory Square Hospital, Washington, Nov. 18th, 1864.
Mitchell, J. H.
Miltimore, Nelson.
McCurdy, Chandlier.
McLaughlin, Thomas G., wounded in action June 17th, 1864; promoted corporal.

Onderdonk, George E., promoted to corporal; wounded June 16th, 1864.
Parker, Francis D., wounded in action June 17th and discharged Dec. 15th, 1864.
Parker, Francis, wounded in action June 18th; promoted Captain company H, 42d Wis., Sept. 23d, 1864.
Peitzke, Wilhelm.
Pitt, Horace C., wounded in action June 18th, 1864.
Reilly, Michael, killed in action June 18th, 1864.
Reilly, Michael O., killed in trenches before Petersburg, July 26th, 1864.
Rush, Thomas, deserted from Camp Randall, Apr. 28th, 1864.
Scott, Stephen.
Scoville, A. H., died in hospital, Washington, D. C., July 15th, '64.
Scoville, Leonard D., killed in action June 18th, 1864.
Shay, Michael, wounded June 17th, 1864.
Shilston, Samuel, wounded in actions June 17th and Aug. 20th, '64.
Shoemaker, Jonathan P., transferred to Vet. Res. Corps.
Smith, Frederick, promoted corporal; wounded Aug. 19th, 1864.
Stolkey, William.
Stone, Samuel H., wounded July 17th, 1864; lost leg Dec. 28th, 1864.
Taff, George, wounded July 30th, 1864.
Thomas, John, deserted from Camp Randall, Apr. 20, 1864.
Toms, George W., wounded July 30th, 1864.
Toomey, Michael, wounded June 17th, 1864.
Tuttle, Peter H., killed in action June 17th, 1864.
Vanderwarker, Frank, discharged for disability.
Wallace, David.
Warren, James, wounded on picket, Jan. 1st, 1865.
Weigal, Jacob, wounded in action, June 17th, 1864.
Winings, John Y.
Willard, David B., wounded June 17th, 1864.
Wojahn, Wilhelm, killed in action, June 18th, 1864.
Young, Aaron, killed in action, June 17th, 1864.
Zahn, William, wounded June 17th, 1864; promoted corporal.
Gleason, Michael, Jr., wounded June 17th, 1864; prom. corporal.

Recruits.

(None.)

Drafted Men.

Joseph Amen.
Fred. Bohren.
P. J. Deuster.
Jos. Hildebrand.
M. Hewitt.
P. Kissinger.
Edw. Lilliecrap.
M. Marquarts.
L. D. Marshall, killed April 2d, 1865.
S. Neville.
August Otto.
Orange Snell.
Fred. Sattler.
John Sieger.
Jos. Smith.
C. N. Clough.
Martin Pfeifer.
Jos. Schineat.

Substitutes.

Dav. Bartle,
Jos. Ergel,
Hy. Eckel,
Wm. Roberts,

Jas. Riley,
Jacob Schneider,
Wiley Whicher,
Cyrus Tucker.

MUSTER ROLL OF "C" COMPANY.

Raised in Mineral Point and neighborhood, by JOHN GREEN and A. J. PARKER. Mustered into U. S. service at Madison, Wisconsin, by Capt. T. T. BRAND, U. S. A., April 13th, 1864.

Captain.

JOHN GREEN. Promoted Major, Oct. 19th; Lieut. Col., Dec. 15th, 1864; and Colonel, July 21st, 1865.

First Lieutenant.

A. J. PARKER. Discharged for physical disability, Nov. 30th, 1864.

Second Lieutenant.

FREEMAN B. RIDDLE. Killed in action, June 17th, 1864.

Sergeants.

Philip Lawrence, promoted 2d Lieut., Dec. 13th, 1864; 1st Lieut., Jan. 9th, 1865; resigned, June 3d, 1865.
W. H. Green, died of wounds, July 9th, 1864.
Francis Cooper, wounded, July 30th.
Wm. Green, promoted 2d Lieut., Jan. 9th, 1865.
Geo. F. Goldthorpe.

Corporals.

Thomas Parkin.
Benson Hall, wounded, July, 30th, 1864; discharged May 19th, 1865.
Sam'l Kenyon.
Dexter B. Spears, wounded, June 17th, 1864.
Oliver Martin.
Reuben D. Shaw.
Charles E. Clark, wounded, June 17th, 1864; died July 7th, 1864:
Thos. W. Argue, died in hospital.

Musicians.

Josiah Baker.
John L. Harrison.

Privates.

Ace, Elijah S.
Argue, John J.
Averill, William.
Benton, John, discharged for disability.
Ball, Julian, deserted, April 26th, 1864.
Baker, Bryant, killed, June 18th, 1864.

Barret, David.
Bryant, David Z.
Clark, Albert B.
Colegrove, Webster, died in hospital, June 17th, 1864.
Cotton, Chas. W.
Crocker, Andrew E., died of wounds received in action, July 10th, 1864.
Cunningham, Henry H., wounded, July 30th.
Cutshall, Taylor.
Day, Albert L.
Domey, Henry, killed, April 2d, 1865.
Estee, John, killed, April 2d, 1865.
Evens, Bow Devine.
Fuller, Joshua P., killed, July 30th, 1864.
French, Edward E., discharged for disability, Oct. 19th, 1864.
Fruit, Enoch.
Green, Henry P.
Gunderson, Thomas.
Hoare, Jas. A.
Hall, Hosea.
Hogness, Matthias, G., died in hospital, Sept. 14th, 1864.
Hollister, W.
Kilmer, Abram.
Kile, Jas.
Kile, Geo. M.
Lemcbe, Adolphe, wounded, June 17th, 1864.
Levings, Noah.
Martin, John.
O'Bryan, John.
Page, Lewis, wounded, June 17th, 1864; discharged, Feb. 20th, 1865.
Paulsen, Kittle, wounded, June 17th, 1864; discharged, Dec. 15th, 1864.
Plummer, Abram.
Pergoy, Nathaniel, died of wounds received in action, July 30th, 1864.
Quimby, Wm., discharged, Aug. 15th, 1864.
Rasey, Francis, H., died of wounds received in action, June 17th, 1864.
Reesman, Phillip.
Ross, Otis, killed in action, June 18th, 1864.
Soper, A., wounded, June 17th, 1864.
Scott, A., died, May 29th, 1864.
Sherwood, D. A., promoted corporal, and 1st sergeant.
Seeley, Stewart.

Smith, Wilber S.
Smith, Benj. F.
Scherer, Nicholas.
Sharer, A., wounded, June 17th, 1864.
Shrider, H.
Spaulding, L.
Spears, Jas.
Spears, Wm. R., discharged, Aug. 25th, 1864.
Teasdale, John.
Terguson, Ole, wounded, July 18th, 1864.
Walker, Peter, died from wounds received in action, June 18th, 1864.
Warren, Frank.
Whitford, John F.
Wheelock, Eugene, killed in action, July 20th, 1864.
Williams, Thos. R., died in hospital, July 13th, 1864.
Wilkinson, Edw.
Woods, Benjamin, prisoner of war, exchanged, Sept., 1864.
Wood, Chas., died in hospital of wounds, received in action, July 19th, 1864.
Webster, Francis A., died in hospital, July 19th, 1864.
Fitch, Vicor.

Recruits.

Schuck, George.
Gaylord, Benj., discharged, June 3d, 1865.
Evins, Abram.
Gardner, Eugene.

Drafted Men.

Bendickson, Knaudt.
Engbertson, Gilbert.
Gunderson, John.
Johnson, Aroe, discharged, Jan. 20th, 1865.
Ormson, Torge.
Oleson, Isaac, discharged, June 3d, 1865.
Oleson, Knaudt.
Cram, Vasco, discharged, June 3d, 1865.
Haas, Matthias.
Kobernos, Fred., discharged, June 3d, 1865.
Krooger, Christian.
Lagerman, Josh, discharged, June 3d, 1865.
Marquite, Frederick.
Kriel, Paulus.
Stolbe, Frederick.

Substitutes.

Cloos, John. Dettenthaler, Fred.
Milling, Paul.

MUSTER ROLL OF "D" COMPANY.

Raised in Waushara and Dane counties by ALVAH NASH and FRANK MUNGER, and mustered into U. S. service at Madison, Wis.

Captain.

ALVAH NASH. Promoted Major, July 21st, 1865.

First Lieutenant.

FRANK J. MUNGER. Prisoner of war, July 30th, 1864. Promoted Captain, July 21st, 1865.

Second Lieutenant.

W. C. POPE. Died of disease, April 30th, 1864.

Sergeants.

Geo. Hurst, promoted 2d Lieut., July 7th, 1864; transferred to company A.
Geo. W. Gustin, died June 3d, 1865.
Jas Bennett, wounded July 30th, 1864.
Caleb Greenfield, wounded June 18th, 1864; discharged March, 1865.
Thompson P. Crowe, wounded Sept. 30th, 1864.

Corporals.

Dan. C. Eager, died of wounds received in action June 17th, 1864.
John W. Jobe.
Joel Dewel, killed July 27th, 1864.
Davis R. Lane, wounded July 30th, 1864; prisoner of war, April 2d, 1865.
Geo. B. Shumway, killed in action June 17th, 1864.
Warren J. Vantassell.
Chas. H. Pynchon.
Zachariah Westbrooke, taken prisoner July 30th and died at Danville, Va.

Musicians.

Fred. Hurst. Benj. Wiggins.

Privates.

Ames, Nathaniel W.
Abbott, Sheridan J., discharged Oct. 19th, 1864.
Angier, Oscar F
Brunton, John, wounded June 18th, 1864.
Bryant, J. M., wounded June 28th, 1864; transferred to V. R. C.
Bromaghim, Geo. W.

Bromaghim, Frank W.
Bent, Wm., wounded Oct. 27th, 1864; discharged June 10th, '65.
Briggs, Wm. H., wounded April 21, 1865; discharged June 6th, 1865.
Blakesly, Tobias L.
Benjamin, Herbert, wounded June 18th, 1864.
Beatty, Wm., wounded June 18th, 1864.
Casey, Amos.
Chase, Jonathan.
Cox, Frederick.
Crawford, Robt. M., prisoner of war, July 30th, 1864.
Cunningham, Chas. F., prisoner of war, July 30th, 1864.
Dallas, John P., prisoner of war, July 30th, 1864.
Douglas, David C., prisoner of war, April 2d, 1865.
Eagan Michael, died while home on furlough, Sept. 26th, 1864.
Eagan, John.
Eager, Thomas, killed in action July 30th, 1864.
Ferdon, Martin O.
Fryman, Jas. D., wounded June 20th, 1864; transf. to V. R. C.
Gillett, Elihu R., died in hospital May 10th, 1864.
Gifford, Jas. M.
Greenfield, John W., transf. to V. R. C.
Harmon, Albion, died in hospital July 5th, 1864.
Hawes, Ed. M.
Hayward, Frauklin, died in hospital Oct. 5th, 1864.
Herrick, S. J.
Hills, Eber H., died in hospital May 7th, 1864.
Holmer, Benj.
House, Elijah, tranferred to 38th Wis. Vol. Infantry.
Howe, Ambrose, wounded June 28th, 1864.
Hurst, Charles, died in hospital Sept. 29th, 1864.
Jameson, James W.
Jameson, Francis, discharged July, 1864.
Jarvis, Willard, wounded July 30th, 1864.
Johnson, John, transferred to 38th Wis. Vol. Infantry.
Joslin John W., promoted 2d Lieut. Dec. 29th, 1864; resigned June 10th, 1865.
King, James, died in hospital May 14th, 1864.
Lamb, Waldo W.
Mills, Noah, died in hospital Aug. 5th, 1864.
Newhall, Harrison C.
Prutzman, David, promoted to 2d Lieut. and killed June 28th, '64.
Putnam, Lyman, wounded June 17th, 1864; died in hospital Aug. 12th, 1864.
Putnam, Jacob, wounded July 30th, 1864, and April 2d, 1865.

Prentice, Nathan B., Q. M. Sergeant; promoted Regimental Q. M., May, 1865.
Ramsbottom, Jas. E.
Readman, Hiram W., transferred to 38th Wis. Vol. Infantry.
Robinson, Ezra B., wounded July 30th, 1864; disc. Sept. 10th, '64.
Schofield, Jacob A.
Seely, Wm.
Short, Patrick.
Shower, John A.
Signor, Jonah.
Smith, Wm., transferred to Vet. Res. Corps.
Specht, Fred., died in prison at Danville, Va., Nov. 3d, 1864.
Stewart, Elisha J., discharged March 24th, 1865.
Stilwell, Clark L., wounded June 17th, 1864.
Taplin, John F.
Wager, Marcus, died of wounds received in action June 17th, '64.
Wagner, Michael.
Waite, William, wounded June 18th, 1864.
Winslow, Elijah.
Young, John, discharged Jan. 10th, 1865.

Recruits—(volunteers.)

Nash, Locey A.
Jones, Sandford G.
Pease, John A.
McMullen, John.
Ditzen, Jacob, discharged June 6th, 1865.
Horats, John, killed in action April 2d, 1865.
Brown, Wm.
Moorhouse, Robert.
Taylor, Andrew M.
Woodward, John B.
Firman, Jacob B.
Hills, Wm. H., wounded in camp, March 27th, 1864.

Drafted.

Wm. Covell.
Richard E. Davis.
Michael Hoose, wounded in action, April 2d, 1865.
Worden A. Wood.
Wm. Hartwig.
Jacob Myers.
Christian Emory.
Adolph Campman.
Charles Nack.

Wm. Kaunie.
Wm. Shrader.
Anton Maas.
Thomas Seholtec.
Charles Block.
Lucus Bartler.
Fred. Harnees.
William Rhineea.

Substitute.

Kelsin Holman, prisoner of war, April 2d, 1865.

MUSTER ROLL OF "E" COMPANY.

Raised in La Crosse and Fond du Lac, by FRANK A. COLE and LEWIS U. BEALL, and mustered into U. S. service, at Madison, Wisconsin, April 18th, 1864.

Captain.

FRANK A. COLE. Died of wounds received in action, July 30th, 1864.

First Lieutenant.

LEWIS U. BEALL. Wounded in action, July 30th, 1864; promoted Captain, Nov. 11th, 1864; honorably discharged, June 10th, 1865.

Second Lieutenant.

MELVILLE A. BARRY. Resigned, Aug. 24th, 1864.

Sergeant.

Archibald Douglas, died of wounds received in action, July 30th, 1864.
Jared Hunstinger, wounded, June 21st, 1864.
Thomas Bishop, died of wounds received in action, June 17th, 1864.
Dan'l Waltz, died in hospital, Jan. 3d, 2865.
D. W. Osbourn, wounded in action, June 18th, 1864.

Corporals.

Wm. Fletcher, died in hospital.
E. Laflin, wounded, June 18th, 1864.
S. Thompson, wounded in action, Aug. 19th, 1864.
A. Terry.
Joseph Kennedy, killed in camp by the fall of a tree, March 16th, 1865.
George Davis, died in hospital, Sept. 21st, 1864.
J. W. Shadbolt.
Wm. Meinzer, killed in action, July 30th, 1864.

Musicians.

Samuel A. Halleck.
T. Brandon.

Privates.

Adam, Abraham.
Baier, Joseph A.
Baldwin, Wm. H., wounded, Sept. 30th, 1864.

Batus, Adam, taken prisoner, July 30th, 1864.
Bowell, Isaac, died in prison, date unknown.
Boyer, Moses, killed in action, June 18th, 1864.
Bresel, Nirum.
Brightman, Wendell D., killed in action, July 30th, 1864.
Briggs, Robt. L., died in hospital at Danville, Va., prisoner, July 30th, 1864.
Brown, Adolphus.
Buck, Cassius M.
Buck, Wm. W., promoted 2d Lieut., Jan. 8th, 1865, Captain, June, 1865.
Carter, Henry E., discharged, May 30th, 1865.
Combs, Jas. W., died in hospital, Aug. 14th, 1864.
Comstock, Marinus, died in hospital at Madison.
Davenport, Nelson, wounded, June 18th, 1864.
Delong, Wm., discharged, Oct. 20th, 1864.
Earl, Thomas, promoted sergeant, Oct. 1st, 1864; wounded, June 18th, 1864; promoted, Lieutenant, July 21st, 1865.
Fawver, Aaron.
Fuller, Jas. L.
Fuller, Levi, wounded, June 18th, 1864; transferred to V R. C., Jan. 17th, 1865.
Gillett, Cyrus B., died in Madison, Wis.
Green, Wm., missing in action, June 18th, 1864; supposed killed.
Gunter, Wm., died in hospital, April 16th, 1865.
Hawes, Lewis M., promoted to chaplain, Aug. 8th, 1864; resigned, March, 1865.
Hall, George, prisoner of war, Dec. 10th, 1864.
Hickman, Albert C., reported killed; missing since July 30th, 1864.
Hopkins, Edmund R.
Huntsinger, Chester, wounded, June 25th, 1864.
Ingalls, Lester H., missing, July 30th, 1864; supposed dead.
Inman, Hiram C.
Johnson, Henry.
Kimball, Wm., deserted, April, 1864.
Larkins, Jas., died of wounds received in action, July 30th, 1864.
Losselyoung, John, missing in action, July 30th, 1864; dead.
Losey, Isaac.
Marshall, John I., killed in action, June 18th, 1864.
Moran, Alf. P., discharged, Jan. 12th, 1865.
Murphy, Michael, discharged, Sept. 26th, 1864.
McCraney, John T.
McKeavey, John.
McLaughlin, James.
Newcomb, Jeremiah.

Nichols, Edgar, wounded in action, June 18th, 1864.
Osier, Joseph, wounded, June 18th, died, July 16th, 1864.
Paulley, Jacob.
Partridge, Edw. B., killed in action, June 18th, 1864.
Peter, August, wounded in action, June 18th, 1864.
Raymond, Geo.
Ritchie, Wesley, wounded in action, July 30th, 1864; transferred to V. R. C.
Shadbolt, R.
Shadbolt, John W.
Smith, Willard.
Sprague, Beriah D., died in hospital, Oct. 20th, 1864.
Sweeney, Wm. A.
Stoops, John.
Terry, Albert O.
Thomas, John, wounded in action, July 17th, 1864.
Thompson, Wm. H.
Thompson, John, killed in action, June 17th, 1864.
Thompson, Charles B., killed in action, June 17th, 1864.
Toothman, Wm., deserted at Madison.
Turner, Abraham.
Waltz, Dan'l, died in hospital, Jan. 3d, 1865.
Watson, Joseph L., transferred to V. R. C.
Watson, Ebenezer, taken prisoner, Dec. 10th, 1864; discharged, May 24th, 1865.
Webster, Bradley.
Wheeler, Ira B., promoted corporal, January, 1865.
Wilkson, Chas.
White, Charles, wounded, June 20th, 1864.
Walker, Alexander.

Recruits—1864.

Edward, Phillip.
Campbell, Albert L., discharged, June 6th, 1865.
Seward, Joel, discharged, June 6th, 1865.
Whipple, Wm. H., discharged, June 6th, 1865.
Van Alstine, Wm., discharged, June 6th, 1865.

Recruits—1865.

Green, Stephen.
Cox, Edward.
Milberon, Peter.
Lynch, Patsy.
Boyce, James.
Perry, Hopkins.
Zander, Lucian V.
Zander, James L.

Substitutes.

Reinschneider, Albert.
Gleason, Burrell.
Dudley, Julius.
Berry, Henry W.

Drafted.

Eighme, Elmer.
Edwards, Henry S.
Merchant, Alexander.
Rosbrook, Jonathan.
Shovey, Peter C.
Bowvee, Henry.
Ecke, Harman.
Ecke, Fred, died in hospital, May, 22d, 1865.
Goltner, Ernste.
Glynn, Timothy.
Maynard, Allen, discharged, June 6th, 1865.
Miller, William.
Stille, Anton.
Schele, Adolph.

MUSTER ROLL OF "F" COMPANY.

Raised in Pierce and Dane counties by E. BURNETT and JAS. C. SPENCER, and mustered into U. S. service at Madison, Wis., April 19th, 1864.

Captain.

ELLSWORTH BURNETT. Promoted Brevet Major, July, 21st, 1864.

First Lieutenant.

JAS. C. SPENCER. Promoted Captain company G, January, 1865, Resigned June, 1865.

Second Lieutenant.

H. W. BELDEN. Promoted 1st Lieut. company A, November 10th, 1864, and Captain company C, Dec. 29th, 1864.

Sergeants.

W. M. Howes, killed in action, April 2d, 1865.
John Butcher, died of wounds received in action, June 18th, 1864.
Geo. W. Chinnoc, transferred to V. R. C.
Morris W. Bliss, killed in action, July 30th, 1864.
Wm. Hasson, promoted sergeant, November 1st, 1864, 2d Lieut., January 8th, 1865.

Corporals.

John H. Gouldsburry, discharged November, 1864.
Jas. Little, killed in action, July 30th, 1864.
Wm. H. Hill, killed in action, July 30th, 1864.
Jos. A. Rollins.
W. T. Bradshaw.
Charles Randall, died May 24th, 1865.
John W. Hilleburt, killed in action, June 18th, 1864.

Musicians.

Brandon,. Taylor.   Slightam, William E.

Privates.

Adams, Lorenzo.
Appleman, Valentine E.
Atchison, John, transferred to Navy.
Bagley, Trueman, died insane, February 18th, 1865.
Barsanter, Frank.
Brown, Charles D.
Burdick, Oscar, killed in action, June 17th, 1864.
Carr, Thomas, Jr.
Caas, George, died of wounds received in action, July 30th, 1864

Carleton, Hollis D., wounded June 17th, 1864, tnd July 30th, 1864.
Cline, George J., promoted corporal January 1st, 1865; killed in action, April 2d, 1865.
Cragan, John, wounded June 18th, 1864; disch. May 3d, 1865.
Coddington, John W., wounded July 30th, 1864.
Conant, Wallace, killed in action, June 18th, 1864.
Douglas, Archibald, transferred to company E.
Davis, James L.
Douglas, John T., prisoner of war, July 30th, 1864.
Dunn, Payson.
Flick, Marion, wounded in action, Sept. 30th, 1864.
Forsythe, Charles R., killed in action, June 17th, 1864.
Fuller, William E.
Gordon, Gardner L., died in hospital, Sept. 7th, 1864.
Graham, Sam., wounded July 30th, 1864; died in prison.
Gray, Alonzo.
Gamble, David.
Hampton, John C., wounded in action, July 30th; discharged June 27th, 1865.
Hayter, William P.
Hazen, Jonathan S.
Hill, Denison K., wounded June 18th, 1864; discharged May 27th, 1865.
Hizer, Adolph, wounded July 30th, 1864.
Hoey, Dennison, prisoner of war, July 30th, 1864; died in prison.
Hodgson, Albert.
Hodgson, G. W., discharged October 17th, 1864.
Houston, George, killed on picket, June 26th, 1864.
Hughhart, James S., discharged May 3d, 1865.
Jones, Evans W., killed June 26th, 1864.
Love, Jeremiah.
Mace, Jonathan.
Maud, William.
McMahan, Peter, wounded July 30th, 1864, and April 2d, 1865.
Morgan, Thomas, wounded June 18th, 1864; disch. Jan. 5th, 1865.
McFail, Neil, wounded June 18th, 1864.
Oleson, Lars, prisoner of war July 30th, 1864; died in prison.
Osgood, Charles J., wounded June 17th, 1864; discharged Dec. 2d, 1864.
Perkins, Benjamin, dismissed by sentence of G. C. M.
Patterson, William.
Patterson, Robert, discharged May 3d, 1865.
Peterson, Ole, wounded July 30th, 1864.
Powell, William, killed in action, June 17th, 1864.
Pieiei, George.

Pulk, David M.
Rautz, Peter, wounded in action, July 30th, 1864 ; discharged May 26th, 1865.
Selleck, Isaac, killed in action, June 18th, 1864.
Smith, George, wounded in action, July 30th, 1864.
Stanley, James G.
Stokes, Elias.
Van Hosen, Norris, killed on picket, July 22d, 1864.
Velzy, Charles, wounded in action, April 2d, 1865.
Walden, Elisha H., killed July 30th, 1864.
Waldroff, Marion.
Ward, Lemuel J., discharged May 4th, 1865.
Weston, Horatio, promoted corporal, January 1st, and sergeant, April 10th, 1865.
Winchester, Judson, promoted sergeant Jan. 1st, 1865, and 2d Lieut., July, 1865.
Wise, Pembroke V., promoted Sergeant Major, June 22d, 1864, and Captain 31st U. S. C. T.
Whitney, Louis M.

Recruits—1864.

Francis Galbraith, discharged May 20th, 1865.
Wm. H. Hogeboom, discharged May 20th, 1865.
Jas. H. Hogeboom, discharged June 6th, 1865.
David C. Martin, promoted sergeant, January 1st, 1865 ; discharged May 20th, 1865.
Ed. W. Sargent, discharged May 24th, 1865.

1865.

Hoefner, Geo., died of wounds received in action, April 2d, 1865.
John Ingraham.
Jacob Miller.
Edwin Slaght.
George Ottman.
Charles Hopkins.
Cortez B. Taylor.
Samuel Barker.

Substitutes.

Rufus H. Holt.
John McFall.
C. J. Midgely.
N. E. McLaughlin.
Patrick Lee.

Drafted.

Thomas Chambers, died in hospital, June 14th, 1865.
John Lynn, died of wounds received in action, April 2d, 1865.
John Shirden.
Norman Shaver, wounded in action, April 2d, 1865.
Fred. Conrad.
John Deits.
Gottlieb Fisher.
E. V. Graves.
Christian Kolberg.
Thomas Metlam.
Henry Rhodes.
Casper Schubert.
Lafayette Saunders.
Henry Sherman.
Charles Silla.
Edward Ward.
A. J. Wood, died in hospital, February 9th, 1865.

MUSTER ROLL OF "G" COMPANY.

Captain.

MARTIN W. HELLER. Discharged for disability, Oct., 1864.

First Lieutenant.

WM. P. ATWELL. Wounded, July 30th, 2864; discharged, Oct., 1864.

Second Lieutenant.

A. J. HOLMES. Taken prisoner, July 30th, 1864; promoted to 1st Lieut. Co. K, June, 1865.

Sergeants.

George Graham, commissioned 1st Lieut., December 29th, 1864.
Stephen Skeel, appointed 1st Serg't Sept., 1st, 1864; commissioned 2d Lieut., March 1st, 1865.
Edward L. Doolittle, wounded and taken prisoner, July 30th, 1864; appointed 1st Serg't March 1st, 1865.
Henry A. Chase, wounded July 30th, 1864; made Commissary Sergeant, Feb. 13th, 1865.
William Thatcher.

Corporal.

William E. Hussey, wounded July 30th, 1864; killed, April 2d, 1865.
Lawrence T. Bristol, killed July 30th, 1864.
Heman A. Babcock, 3d Corp., promoted 1st Serg't company D.
John M. Cenru, killed July 30th, 1864.
George H. Vaughan, killed July 30th, 1864.
Ozias C. Dwyer, made Serg't Jan. 1st, 1865.
Robert R. Minnick.
Benjamin M. Collins, reduced to the ranks.

Privates.

James E. Andrews, promoted Corporal, August 1st, 1864; made Sergeant, March 1st, 1865.
Thomas Applebee.
William Arthurs.
Robert A. Amor, died October 22d, 1864.
George N. Bishop.
Christian Bergeman, killed July 30th, 1864.
Seneca Bentley, deserted June 14th, 1864.
James H. Bellinger.
Albert Bovee, Jr.
Charles B. Babcock, promoted Corporal May 2d, 1865.
Franklin Bigelow, killed July 30th, 1864.

Orlando A. Burdick, wounded July 30th, 1864.
Samuel M. Badger.
Francis A. Baldwin.
Thomas Curtin,.killed July 30th, 1864.
Francis Cain.
George Cole, deserted June, 1864.
Hiram P. Cutting, prisoner of war since July 30th, 1864.
Joseph E. Clark.
George Daggett, died August 19th, 1864.
Horatio N. Day.
Elias Delong, discharged May 27th, 1865.
Alfred Dewitt.
Thomas S. Draper.
John Farnsworth, died in prison at Danville, Va.
Victor Fitch, transferred to company C.
Egbert Gardner, wounded July 30th, 1864.
Jens Holsteenson.
Isaac Joiner, transferred to V. R. C.
Thomas H. Lea, killed July 30th, 1864.
John Loible, wounded April 2d, 1865.
Nicholas H. Lang, killed July 30th, 1864.
Orange M. Lincoln, killed July 30th, 1864.
Edmund M. Long, killed July 24th, 1864, on picket.
Miron E. Lawrence, promoted Corporal, May 1st, 1865.
Joseph H. Meixell, transferred to V. R. C.
John McIntyre, promoted Corporal, March 1st, 1865.
Luther L. Masser.
Charles Nickell, killed Sept. 30th, 1864.
Charles J. Neff, killed July 30th, 1864.
George W. Pitt, wounded on picket July 23d, 1864.
Adolphus Page, killed July 30th, 1864.
Minn Palmer, killed July 30th, 1864.
William Paine, deserted December, 1864.
Isaac J. Paine.
John A. Plunkett, taken prisoner July 30th, 1864.
David Pearson, deserted May, 1864.
Mortimer W. Perry, killed April 2d, 1865.
Clarence L. Powers, promoted Corporal, April 1st, 1865.
Freeman L. Roberts.
George Right, deserted May, 1864.
Richard B. Rose.
Charles Salisbury, wounded himself January 3d, 1865.
Josiah Sweet, discharged May 27th, 1865.
Justin L. Spencer.
John Milton Smith, wounded July 30th, 1864.

John Smith, deserted May, 1864.
Francis Schofield, died June 14th, 1864.
William Shilling, wounded April 2d, 1865.
Henry R. Sprage, died at Danville, Va., in prison. .
Wilton L. Squires.
Joseph H. Sexton, promoted Corporal, Feb. 12th, 1865.
James Q. Severns, promoted Corporal, June 6th, 1864.
James J. Taylor, promoted Sergeant, April 1st, 1865.
Theodore T. Upright, killed July 30th, 1864.
Meredith M. Whitt, transferred to company H.
Hans. B. Warner, wounded July 30th, 1864, and taken prisoner.
William Wells, died October 14th, 1864.
Edward Youereil, wounded July 30th, 1864.
George Banon.

Volunteer Recruits.

John A. Showns, transferred to company D.
Robert Patchet.
John Cummings.
William Woolfitt, Jr.
John Deniger.
Cyrus Widger.
Patrick Penneffy.
Monmouth Baldwin.
James Bond.
John McGeen.
Van Vechten Livingston.

Drafted Recruits.

Stephen Griffith, wounded April 2d, 1865.
Charles P. Rood.
Andrew Matlott.
Nicholas Rottice.
Daniel Kennedy.
Miles Smith.
Joseph Shermer.
Michael Shultz.
Olois Schafer.
Peter Vroman.
Christopher Winkauf, promoted Corporal, May 1st, 1865.
John Dunck.
Freerick Ellion.
Robert Kencel.
Frederick Ohen, wounded April 2d, 1865.
Martin Van-de-Vel-de.

Substitutes.

Nels Bryngleson, wounded April 2d, 1865.
William H. Rood.
Joseph Dupoint, wounded April 2d, 1865.
Marius Pero, killed December 22d, 1864.
John H. Dalton.
Edwin C. Rist.
Thomas Feenan.
Jacob Goodrow.

MUSTER ROLL OF COMPANY "H."

PERMANENT PARTY.

Captain.

FRANK T. HOBBS. Wounded, June 18th, 1864.

First Lieutenant.

THOS. CARMICHAEL. Discharged, Oct. 7th, 1864.

Second Lieutenant.

JOS. H. BRIGHTMAN. Resigned, Aug. 7th, 1864.

Sergeants.

John Deidrich.
Carl M. Peck, killed in action, June 18th, 1864.
Hy. Carman.
D. L. Cole, killed in action, June 17th, 1864.
Edw. Ehle, promoted.

Corporals.

Fred. Bassett, prisoner of war, July 30th, 1864.
R. M. Stockwell.
Jas. B. Wait.
A. Plummer, discharged, July 3d, 1864.
Chauncey Blunt.
S. P. Kanable, Prisoner of war, July 30th, 1864; promoted, Serg't, May 1st, 1865.
John M. Wells, promoted 1st Serg't, Jan. 1st, 1865; prisoner of war, April 2d, 1865.
Chas. Schrœder, wounded, June 18th, 1864.

Musician.

Adelbert Eastman, discharged. March 25th, 1865.

Privates.

Althouse, Christian.
Ackley, Adnah, promoted corporal, April 11th, 1865.
Allabeck, Geo. W.
Arnald, Edw'd.
Behling, Geo. W. P.
Baird, Jas. R.
Bendrick, John, killed in action, June 18th, 1864.
Boyle, Patrick.
Benscotter, Barney.

Becker, Henry D.
Bassett, Frederick, promoted corporal, May 1st, 1864; prisoner, July, 30th.
Blunt, Chauncey.
Bandel, Joseph, promoted, 2d Lieut., Jan. 8th, 1865.
Beden, Jonas W.
Chisholm, Wm.
Clinkamer, Peter, died of wounds, Aug. 3d, 1864.
Crouse, Jonathan.
Core, Geo. W., promoted corporal, Jan. 1st, 1865.
Crabtree, John, died of wounds, Nov. 8th, 1865.
Dillen, Abraham, prisoner of war, April 2d, 1864.
Endicott, Wm. A., killed in action, April 2d, 1865; promoted sergeant, Jan. 1st, 1865.
Ericson, Lewis M., promoted corporal, April 11th, 1865.
Foss, Charles B.
Gould, Charles H., killed in action, June 18th, 1864.
Gillett, Marcus D., died of wounds received in action, July 20th, 1864.
Gault, Henry A., killed in action, April 2d, 1865.
Hughbanks, David, deserted, May 2d, 1864.
Hoke, George.
Heath, Orin.
Highday, Geo. S.
Halsted, Luther.
Kendal, Zachariah, discharged, March 6th, 1865.
Kanable, Simon, promoted sergeant, May 1st; prisoner of war, July, 30th, 1864.
Hassilky, Wm., killed in action, June 18th, 1864.
Lamb, Wm. A.
Long, Thomas, died of wounds, July 6th, 1864.
Luchterhaud, Ernst, died of wounds, July 9th, 1864.
Manlove, Oliver P., prisoner of war, July 30th, 1864.
Metcalf, Wm. G., discharged, March 25th, 1865.
McCloud, Duley, killed in action, June 18th, 1864.
Nash, Anderson.
Norton, Edward L.
Prince, Sandford C.; discharged, July 5th, 1864.
Parvis, Geo. W., promoted, April 11th, 1865.
Provo, Thos., prisoner, July 30th, 1864,
Parker, Rodolpho W., transferred to V. R. C.
Quick, Riley.
Rowe, Geo., promoted corporal, May 1st, 1865.
Reece, Chas. H., discharged, July 3d, 1864.
Soper, Foster R., died, Aug., 1864.

Safford, Wm.
Schrœder, Charles, died of wounds, July 6th, 1864.
Schrœder, Charles, promoted corporal; wounded, June 18th, 1864.
Statton, Wm., discharged, March 25th, 1865.
Slonager, Fred., died of wounds, July 24th, 1864.
Skinner, Wm.
Skinner, Abner, B., promoted corporal, May 1st, 1865.
Scheidigger, Andrew, promoted corporal, Jan. 1st, 1865.
Scoville, Levi.
Storey, John W.
Trigel, Reichart, killed in action.
Thorpe, Thomas E., transferred to V. R. C.
Willoughby, John R., died of wounds received, Sept. 12th, 1864.
Winfield, Henry.
Wood, Aseill, killed in action, July 30th, 1864.
Wells, John M., 1st Serg't, Jan. 1st, 1865; prisoner of war, April 2d, 1865.
Wagner, John.
Dickey, Rob't.
Dean, Lafayette, discharged, Nov. 18th, 1864.
Flook, Abner H., transferred to V. R. C.
Lee, John, deserted, May 2d, 1864.
Paine, Wm. A.
Deiderich, John.
Peck, Carl M., killed in action, June 18th, 1864.
Carman, Henry.
Cole, David L., killed in action, June 17th, 1864.
Ehle, Edw. A., promoted sergeant.
Stockwell, Rob't M.
Wait, Jas. B., promoted corporal, May 1st, 1864.
Plumer, Amos, discharged, July 3d, 1864.

Recruits.

Appleman, Valentine E., discharged, Jan. 23d, 1865.
Maud, Wm., discharged, Jan. 23d, 1865.
Tax, Thos.
Belknap, Seba.
Tax, Geo.
Pottgeisser, Phillip.
Warwick, Dan'l.
Sercom, Chas.

Drafted.

Schmitt, Wm.
Schuster, Christian.
Bosak, Wm., killed in action, April 2d, 1865.
Kitzman, John F.
Kruyer, Dan'l.
Kreuke, Charles.
Mallo, Fred., killed in action, April 2d, 1865.
Burchardt, Chas.
Luther, Paul.
Dollert, Carol.
Kowitz, Andrew.
Joercs, Thomas, discharged, May 20th, 1865.
Wollenberg, Fred.
Schultz, Herman.
Wintermantel, Jacob.
Lumbay, Fred.
Tarvour, John.
Gasser, Geo.
Gallis, John.
Gelhaus, Arnold.
Sehard, Necklaus, discharged, March 6th, 1865.

MUSTER ROLL OF "I" COMPANY.
Raised in various counties.

Captain.

GEORGE A. BECK.

First Lieutenant.

EDWARD HANSON. Resigned July 20th, 1864.

Second Lieutenant.

JOSEPH O. CHILSON. Dismissed the service by G. C. M.

Sergeants.

John C. Avery, wounded June 18th, 1864 ; reduced to ranks Jan. 1st, 1865.
Matthias Bauer, discharged October 22d, 1864.
Elias W. Reidy.
John Regan, reduced to the ranks, November 1st, 1864.
Edward Thurston.

Corporals.

Titsworth Barrett, reduced to ranks Nov. 1st, 1864.
Henry Kulman, reduced to ranks Nov. 1st, 1864.
John Stockhardt, killed in action July 30th, 1864.
Louis Dorman.
Seth G. Ferdon, reduced to ranks Nov. 1st, 1864.
E. R. Mavville.
Charles Frank, promoted Sergeant January 1st, 1865.
Joseph Blair.

Musicians.

Privates.

Avery, John C., wounded June 18th, 1864.
Applebee, Gilbert, wounded June 18th, 1864.
Ammerman, Albert.
Allen, Lloyd W., deserted May 23d, 1865.
Brodhagen, William.
Bagg, James, deserted May 1st, 1865.
Bruss, Gottlieb.
Brown, Charles P., died in hospital Nov. 28th, 1864.
Blair, Joseph.
Bates, Aaron G., died of wounds received in action July 30th, '64.
Callahan, Matthew, killed in action July 30th, 1864.
Cowdy, Lester L.
Caldwell, William A., killed in action July 30th, 1864.

Cady, Benjamin A., discharged April 20th, 1865.
Cook, Wm. H., died in hospital September 27th, 1864.
Dipple, Conrad, discharged December 8th, 1864.
Donaldson, Henry.
Fidier, Christian.
Frank, Charles.
Ferdon, Seth.
Fifield, Jacob, killed in action July 30th, 1864.
Ferris, Frank, discharged July 5th, 1864.
Ferris, Newton, discharged June 1st, 1864.
Fendleson, Jones, discharged July 5th, 1864.
Graham, George, transferred to company G.
Goodknow, Austin, died in hospital July 30th, 1864.
Hatch, Lester M.
Hamilton, George M., wounded in action June 17th, 1864; discharged March 18th, 1865.
Harris, Caleb.
Henry, James, deserted May 1st, 1865.
Honey, Henry G.
Johnson, Peter I., wounded in action September 30th, 1864.
Kennedy, Henry, discharged July 5th, 1864.
Kimball, Nathaniel, died of wounds received in action June 17th, 1864.
Klauch, Peter, deserted May 1st, 1864.
Lenz, Ferdinand, discharged June 8th, 1865.
Lease, John J., wounded Sept. 30th, 1864.
Lease, Wm. A., killed in action June 18th, 1864.
Lombard, Halbert, discharged July 5th, 1864.
Mosey, George W., discharged July 5th, 1864.
Moore, Abner M., deserted in battle August 19th, 1864.
Maxin, Zenas, promoted Sergeant, Nov. 1st, 1864; discharged June 20th, 1865.
Mayville, Ephraim.
Musback, Fred., wounded June 18th, 1864.
Myers, Jacob H., died in hospital Oct. 8th, 1864.
Marshal, Hy., mustered out June 27th, 1865.
Pulk, Henry, died of wounds received in action June 18th, 1864.
Parks, Henry S.
Perkins, Wyatt.
Picket, Samuel, promoted Corporal January 1st, 1865 ; Q. M. Sergeant May 1st, 1865.
Qualman, John.
Robertson, Solomon, promoted Corporal November 1st, 1864 ; reduced April 1st, 1865.
Riley, Wesley, wounded July 30th; promoted 1st Sergeant January 1st, 1865 ; 2d Lieutenant March 23d, 1865.

Randall, Albert.
Rappold, Henry, killed in action July 30th, 1864.
Roseman, Henry G., discharged May 3d, 1865.
Schous, Henry, died September 26th, 1864.
Seebor, John W., discharged August 3d, 1864.
Strong, Morell V. G., discharged February 12th, 1865.
Stemper, Nicholas.
Stringer, William.
Staver, Henry.
Winkler, Herman, wounded June 25th, 1864; discharged June 26th, 1865.
Weldon, Elias, discharged July 5th, 1864.
Walt, John.
Warner, Almon.
Wilcox, Seth, died of wounds received in action Sept. 30th, 1864.
Wolcott, David L.
Dahrman, Louis.
Kulman, Henry, wounded July 30th, 1864; disch. May 3d, 1865.
Stockhart, John, died in prison at Danville, Va.
Titsworth, Burrett, promoted Corporal; mustered out May 22d, '65.
Bauer, Matthias.
Reidy, Elias W.
Regan, John, wounded June 18th, 1864.
Thurston, Edward.
Dike, William, deserted May 14th, 1864.
Kellner, Andrew, wounded July 2d, 1864.
Rowley, Newell G., promoted Commissary Sergeant Aug. 1st, '64.
Walker, Alexander.

Recruits, (1865.)

George L. Cross, promoted Sergeant March 30th, 1865.
John H. La Point.
Henry B. Starkey.
Edgar Lyon.
Jacob Thon.
Frank Sowa.
Charles Lauer.

Substitutes.

Henry Winkler.
William Ohlman.
John Lick.
August Herbet.
Mority, Fidler.
Ernst Wagner.

John Wagner.
Charles Louky.
August Knocku.
Rudolph Nauman.
Frank Bernardu.
Ernst Miller.
Hermon Gable.
Carl Nernberger.
Jacob Schindler.
Christoph Henrich.
Anton Mickle, discharged May 3d, 1865.

Drafted.

Joseph Bronson.
Amos Favel.
George Mais.
Bertholde Schwartze.
Joseph Schneider.
George Kopetzka.
Albert Reinschneider.
August Heineman.

MUSTER ROLL OF "K" COMPANY

Raised in Shawanaw, Dane, and other counties, by J. W. HITCHCOCK and THOS. CARMICHAEL. Mustered into U. S. service at Madison, Wis., May 5th, 1864.

Captain.

A. A. BURNETT. Died of wound received in action, July 30th, 1864.

First Lieutenant.

GEO. D. McDILL. Wounded in action, July 30th; promoted Capttain, Sept. 27th; resigned, Nov. 2d, 1864.

Second Lieutenant.

EDW. I. GRUMLEY. Promoted 1st. Lieut., Oct. 19th; transferred to company "H."

Sergeants.

Meredith M. Whitt, wounded and prisoner, July 30th; escaped and promoted 1st Lieut., Dec. 29th, 1864; killed in action, April 2d, 1865.
Clark Thomas, promoted 2d Lieut., Dec. 29th, 1864.
Isaac N. Salisbury, wounded, July 30th, 1864.
Thos. Kershaw, wounded and prisoner, July 30th, 1864.
John Gallaino, killed in action, Aug. 19th, 1864.

Corporals.

Benj. N. Smith.
Wm. Coxball, wounded in action, Aug. 19th; transferred to V. R. C.
Semour Hah-pah-ton-won-i quette, killed in action, July 30th, 1864.
Jervis Ames, wounded in action, Aug. 19th, 1864; discharged, June 11th, 1865.
Peter Little.
Alex. McCurdy.
Joseph Lane, wounded, July 27th, 1864.
Meshell Kayso.

Privates.

Amundson, Halvor.
Ah-she-toh-yash, James, wounded, Aug. 20th, 1864.
Ah-pah-ke, Isaac, wounded, Aug. 20th, 1864.
Bishop, Chester, killed in action, Aug. 21st, 1864.
Bean, Norris.
Chatfield, David B.
Cox, Charles, wounded in action, Aug. 21st, 1864.

Downie, Geo. H., discharged, June 10th, 1865.
Evins, Edward.
Hammond, Lewis P., prisoner of war, July 30th, 1864; died in hospital, March 21st, 1865.
Hah-pah-to-ka-sic, Charles.
Hart, Moses.
Hammond, Abner, deserted, June 26th, 1864.
Holbrook, Geo. F., deserted, July 13th, 1864.
Hillier, Wm. H.
Hopper, Martin S.
Hamblin, Henry S., wounded in action, Aug. 21st, 1864.
Ingalls, Frank H., missing in action, July 30th, 1864.
Ireton, Robert, prisoner of war, July 30th, 1864.
Kah-wah-tah-wah-pao, Hy, wounded, April 2d, 1865.
Kenosha, Meshell, killed in action, July 30th, 1864.
Kah-to-tah, Jerome, wounded in action, July 30th, 1864.
Ken-nein-we-kasic, Samuel.
Kas-kah-tup-pa, William.
King, Peter, wounded in action, July 30th, 1864.
Little, Peter.
Mitchell, Robert R., wounded in action, April 2d, 1865.
McCormick, Patrick.
Murray, Julius A, wounded in action, July 30th, 1865.
May-ohe-won, Jos., deserted.
Mach-me-no-mo nce, Joseph.
Mah ma-ka-wit, Meshel, wounded in action, July 30th, 1864.
Menosh, John, discharged, April 10th, 1865.
Mosh-she nosh, Barney, killed in action, Aug. 21st, 1864.
Mach-o-pah-tah, Solomon.
McGowan, Patrick, prisoner of war, July 30th, 1864; died, March 20th, 1865.
McCurdy, Alexander.
McCurdy, Thomas, deserted.
Non-noc-ke-keshin, Mitchell.
Nab-pah-nah-cochen, deserted, July 12th, 1864.
Nab-she-kah-appah, Amable, killed in action, July 30th, 1864.
Nah-wah-quah, Joseph, killed in action, July 30th, 1864.
Nelson, Gunder, wounded and prisoner, July 30th; died, March 20th, 1865.
Osh-wah-nometon, Meshell, deserted.
Nugent, John, discharged, April 8th, 1865.
Pah-po-not-nien, Peter, prisoner of war, July 30th, 1864; died, March 20th, 1865.
Pe-quach-ena-nien, Jac., wounded in action, July 30th, 1864.
Pah-po-quah, John B., missing in action, July 30th, 1864.

Pah-po-quin, Joseph, killed in action, Aug. 19th, 1864.
Piah-wah-sha, August, prisoner of war July 30th, 1864; died, March 20th, 1865.
Pah-ye-wah-sit, Joseph, wounded in action, Aug. 21st, 1864.
Rubber, Benjamin, died of wounds received in action, July 30th, 1864.
Swenson, John A.
Smith, Noyce B.
Shawano, Lewis.
Sha-boi-sha-ka, Meshell, wounded in action, July 30th, 1864.
Sha-wah-ne-penas, John.
Shah-boi-sha-kah, Meshell, prisoner of war, July 30th, 1864.
She-she-quin, Edward, wounded, Feb. 27th, 1865, in camp.
She-pah-kasic, John B., wounded in action, Aug. 19th, 1864.
Spinney, Wm., wounded, July 30th, 1864; promoted sergeant, Nov. 1st, 1864; 1st Serg't, July, 1865.
Stevens, Chas. E., wounded, July 30th, 1864; discharged, Sept. 12th, 1864.
Salisbury, Isaac N., wounded, July 30th, 1864; discharged Sept. 12th, 1864.
Smith, Benj.
Teco, Dominique, killed in action, July 30th, 1864.
Townsend, Alfred.
Wah-ton-nut, Felix, killed in action, July 30th, 1864.
Wah-bun-o, Antoine, wounded, Aug. 20th, 1864.
Weier-is-kasit, Paul, missing in action, July 30th, 1864.
Waukau, John.
Wah-sah-we-quon, Joseph, prisoner, July. 30th, 1864; died, April 7th, 1865.
Wah-sha-kah-ka-nick, Robert.

Recruits.

Geo. Andree, wounded in action, April 2d, 1864.
Wm. Claus.
Fred. Grimshaw, discharged, June 6th, 1865.
Geo. Kingsbury.
Ralph Lees.
Edw. A. Russell.
Andrew Elliott.

Substitutes.

Andrew Anderson.
Henry Dane.
Martin Drott.
Daniel Large.

Sam'l W. Ringwood.
Joseph Storr.
Chas. C. Troxell.
Thasten Thastenson.
Alfred Hubbard.
Eugene Auchmoody.

Drafted Men.

Ole Christopherson, discharged, June 7th, 1865.
Ole Christopherson, jr., discharged, June 7th, 1865.
Philander H. Cady.
Halbert Harvey.
John Knudson, discharged, June 7th, 1865.
Laban La Rue.
Henry Olson, discharged, June 7th, 1865.
Peter Schwindling.

OUR DEAD.

"A" COMPANY.

Capt. Samuel Stevens, June 18th, 1864.
1st Lieut. Sanford Jones, August 29th, 1864.
Sergt. Oliver H. Hunt, December 16th, 1864.
Corp. Tim. E. Wade, November 7th, 1864.
Corp. Benjamin F. Wheeler, June 18th, 1864.

Privates.

Wm. Jas. Black, July 12th, 1864, from wounds received in action, June 18th, 1864.
John E. Greenhalgh, June 18th, 1864.
Jesse Lane, July 7th, 1864.
Annum Oleson, September 19th, 1864.
John Peak, July 7th, 1864.
John Riner, November 14th, 1864.
Munson B. Sanford, June 18th, 1864.
Walter Scott, June 24th, 1864, killed on picket.
William B. Smith, June 18th, 1864.
Sam. Springer, September 4th, 1864, effect of wounds received in action, June 18th, 1864.
Edward N. Van Deustan, July 30th, 1864.
James L. Warner, June 18th, 1864.
Almond Whitney, June 18th, 1864.

"B" COMPANY.

1st Lieut. Wm. H. Earl, July 4th, 1864, of wounds received in action, June 17th.
Sergt. O. E. Rice, August 14th, 1864, of wounds received in action, July 30th.
Corp. H. G. Brown, August 3d. 1864, of wounds received in action, June 17th.

Privates.

William E. Barnes, November 10th, 1864.
Hollis J. Barnes, Junuary 17th, 1865.
Otis Cross, July 30th, 1864, missing, supposed killed.
John W. Duley, date unknown.
Cyrus R. Eaton, date unknown.
Hugh Finley, June 18th, 1864.
Napoleon Fuller, July 6th, 1864.

John Hall, June 17th, 1864.
John C. Holton, April 27th, 1864.
Hugh Lee, June 24th, 1864.
Fred. Luhm, November 18th, 1864.
Michael Reilly, June 18th, 1864.
Michael O'Reilly, July 26th, 1864.
A. Scoville, July 15th, 1864.
L. D. Scoville, June 18th, 1864.
Peter H. Tullis, June 17th, 1864.
William Wojahn, June 18th, 1864.
A. Young, June 19th, 1864, of wounds received in action, June 17th.

"C" COMPANY.

2d Lieut. F. B. Riddle, June 19th, 1864, of wounds received June 18th.
Sergt. W. H. Green, July 19th, 1864, wounds received June 18th.
Corp. E. Wheelock, July 30th, 1864.
Corp. Chas. E. Clark, July 17th, 1864, wounded in action.
Corp. John W Estee, April 2d, 1865.

Privates.

W Colegrove, June 17th, 1864.
A. E. Crocker, July 10th, 1864, killed on picket.
J. P. Fuller, July 30th, 1864.
M. G. Hogness, September 14th, 1864.
N. Peregoy. July 30th, 1864.
F. H. Rasey, June 18th, 1864.
Otis Ross, June 18th. 1864.
A. Scott, May 29th, 1864.
P. Walker, August 22d, 1864.
Thomas R Williams, July 13th, 1864.
Charles Wood, July 19th, 1864.
F. A. Webster, July 19th, 1864.
T. W Argue, July 19th, 1864.
Henry Domey, April 2d, 1865.

."D" COMPANY.

2d Lieut. Webster C. Pope, April 30th, 1864.
2d Lieut. David Prutzman, June 29th, 1864.
Sergt. George W. Gustin, January 4th, 1865.
Corp. George B. Shumway, June 17th: 1864.
Corp. Joel Denel, July 28th, 1864.
Corp. Daniel C. Eager, July 14th, 1864.
Corp. Franklin Haywood, February 5th, 1864.
Corp. Zachariah Westbroke, November 7th, 1864.

Privates.

James King, May 14th, 1864.
Thomas Eager, July 30th, 1864.
Albion Harmon, July 5th, 1864.
Noah Mills, August 5th, 1864.
Lyman Putnam, August 12th, 1864.
Elihu Gillett, August 10th, 1864.
Eber H. Hills, May 7th, 1864.
Marcus Wager, July 8th, 1864.
Charles Hurst, September 29th, 1864.
Michael Eagan, September 26th, 1864.
Fred. Speck, November 3d, 1864.
John Horats, April 2d, 1865.

"E" COMPANY.

Capt. Frank A. Cole, July 30th, 1864.
1st Sergt. Archibald Douglas, July 30th, 1864.
Sergt. Thomas Bishop, June 17th, 1864.
Sergt. Daniel Waltz, January 3d, 1865.
Corp. William Fletcher.
Corp. Joseph Kennedy, March 16th, 1864, killed by fall of a tree.
Corp. George Davis, September 21st, 1864.
Corp. William Meinzer, July 30th, 1864.

Privates.

T. Bowell, died in rebel prison, date unknown.
Moses Boyer, June 18th, 1864.
W D. Brightman, July 30th, 1864.
R. L. Briggs, Danville, Va., prisoner of war.
James W. Combs, August 14th, 1864.
Marinus Comstock.
C. C. Gillett.
W. Green, June 18th, 1864.
William Gunter, April 16th, 1865.
A. C. Hickman, July 30th, 1864, missing in action.
L. H. Ingalls, July 30th, 1864, missing in action.
James Larkins, July 30th, 1864.
J. I. Marshall, June 18th, 1864.
Joseph Osier, July 16th, 1864, wounded June 18th, 1864.
Beriah Sprague, October 20th, 1864.
John Thompson, June 17th, 1864.
Charles B. Thompson, June 17th, 1864.
Daniel Waltz, January 3d, 1865.
Fred. Eche, May 22d, 1865.

COMPANY "F."

1st Serg't W. M. Howes, April 2d, 1865.
Serg't John Butcher, June 18th, 1864.
Serg't Morris W. Bliss, July 30th, 1864.
Corp. Jas. Little, July 30th, 1864
Corp. Wm. H. Hill, July 30th, 1864.
Corp. Chas. Randall, May 24th, 1864.
Corp. J. W Hilleburt, June 18th, 1864.

Privates.

Truman Bagley, Feb. 18th, 1865.
Oscar Burdick, June 17th, 1864.
Geo. Caas, July 30th, 1864.
Hollis D. Carlton, July 30th, 1864.
Geo. J. Cline, April 2d, 1865.
Wallace Conant, June 18th, 1864.
Chas. R. Forsythe, June 17, 1864.
Gardner, L. Gordon, Sept. 7th, 1864.
Sam. Graham, died in rebel prison.
Dennison Hoey, died in rebel prison.
E. W. Jones, June 26th, 1864.
Lars Oleson, died in rebel prison.
Wm. Powell, June 17th, 1864.
Isaac Selleck, July 30th, 1864.
N. Van Hosen, July 22d, killed on picket.
Elisha H. Walden, July 30th, 1864.
Geo. Houston, June 26th, 1864.
Geo. Hoefner, April 2d, 1864.
Thos. Chambers, June 14th, 1865.
John Lynn, April 2d, 1865.
A. J. Wood, Feb. 9th, 1865.

COMPANY "G."

Corp. Wm. E. Hussey, April 2d, 1865.
Corp. Lawrence J. Bristol, July 40th, 1864.
Corp. John. M. Converse, July 30th, 1864.
Corp. Geo. H. Vaughan, July 30th, 1864.

Privates.

R. A. Amor, Oct. 22d, 1864.
Christian Bergeman, July 30th, 1864.
Frank Bigelow, July 30th, 1864.
Thomas Curtin, July 30th, 1864.
Geo. Daggett, Aug. 19th, 1864.

John Farnsworth, died in prison at Danville, Va.
Thos. H. Lea, July 30th, 1864.
Nicholas H. Lang, July 30th, 1864.
Orange M. Lincoln, July 30th, 1864.
Edmund M. Long, July 24th, 1864; killed on picket.
Charles Nickels, Sept. 30th, 1864.
Chas. I. Neff, July 30th, 1864.
Adolphus Page, July 30th, 1864.
M. Palmer, July 30th, 1864.
M. W. Perry, April 2d, 1865.
F. Schofield, June 14th, 1864.
H. R. Sprague, died in prison at Danville, Va.
Theo. T. Upright, July 30th, 1864.
W. Well, Oct. 14th, 1864.
M. Pero, Dec. 22d, 1864.

COMPANY "H."

Privates

John Bendrick, June 18th, 1864.
P. Clinkamer, Aug. 3d, 1864.
J. Crabtree, Nov. 8th, 1864.
W. A. Endicott, April 2d, 1865.
Chas. H. Gould, June 18th, 1864.
M. D. Gillett, July 20th, 1864.
H. A. Gault, April 2d, 1865.
Wm. Hassilky, June 18th, 1864.
Thos. Long, July 6th, 1864.
Ernst Luchterland, July 9th, 1864.
Dudley McCloud, June 18th, 1864.
Foster R. Soper, Aug., 1864.
Chas. Schrœder, July 6th, 1864.
Fred. Slonager, July 24th, 1864.
Reichart, Trigel, April 2d, 1865.
J. R. Willoughby, Sept. 12th, 1864.
A. Wood, July 30th, 1864.
C. M. Peck, June 18th, 1864.
D. L. Cole, June 17th, 1864.
Wm. Bosack, April, 17th, 1864.
Fred. Mallo, April 2d, 1865.

COMPANY "I."

Corp. John Stockhardt, July 30th, 1864.

Privates.

Gilbert Applebee, June 18th, 1864.
Charles P. Brown, Nov. 28th, 1864; disease.
Aaron G. Bates, July 30th, 1864.
Matthew Callaban, July 30th, 1864.
Wm. A. Caldwell, July 30th, 1864.
Wm. H. Cook, Sept. 27th, 1864; in hospital.
Jacob Fifield, July 30th, 1864.
Austin Goodknow, July 30th, 1864.
Nath. Kimball, June 17th, 1864.
Wm. A. Lease, June 18th, 1864.
J. H. Myres, Oct. 8th, 1864; in hospital.
Henry Pulk, June 18th, 18th, 1864.
Henry Rappold, July 30th, 1864.
Henry Schous, Sept. 26th, 1863.
Seth Wilcox, Sept. 30th, 1864.
John Stockbart, died in rebel prison at Danville, Va.

COMPANY "K."

Capt. A. A. Burnett, Aug. 18th, 1864; wounds received July 30th, 1864.
1st Lieut. Meredith M. Whitt, April 2d, 1865.
Serg't John Gallaino, Aug. 19th, 1864.
Corp. Semour Hah-pah-ton-won-i-quette, July 30th, 1864.

Privates.

Chester Bishop, Aug. 21st, 1864.
Lewis P. Hammond, March 21st, 1865; taken prisoner, July 30th, and died in Washington, shortly after his exchange.
Frank H. Ingalls, July 30th, 1864.
Kenosha Neshell, July 30th, 1864.
Patrick McGowan, March 20th, 1865; prisoner of war, July 30th.
Amable Nah-she-kah-appah, July 30th, 1864.
Joseph Nah-wab-quah, July 30th, 1864.
Gunder Nelson, March 20th, 1865; prisoner of war, July 30th, 1864.
Peter Pah-po-not-nien, March 20th, 1865; prisoner of war, July 30th, 1864.
John B. Pah-po-quah, March 20th, 1865; prisoner of war, July 30th, 1864.

Augtst Piah-wah-sha, March 20th, 1865; prisoner of war, July 30th, 1864.
Joseph Pah-po-quin, Aug. 19th, 1864.
Benj. Rubber, July 30th, 1864.
Meshell Shah-boi-shak-kah, July 30th, 1864.
Dominique Teco, July 30th, 1864.
Felix Wah-to-nut, July 30th, 1864.
Paul Weier-is-kasit, July 30th, 1864.
Joseph Wah sha-we-quon, July 30th, 1864.

ROSTER OF THE 37TH WIS. VOLS.

AT ITS FINAL MUSTER OUT.

COLONEL.		LIEUT. COLONEL.
JOHN GREEN.		R. C. EDEN.
MAJOR.	ADJUTANT.	QUARTERMASTER.
ALVAH NASH.	C. I. MILTIMORE.	N. D. PRENTISS.
SURGEON.	1ST ASSISTANT.	2D ASSISTANT.
D. C. ROUNDY.	J. H. ORRICK.	Vacant.

LINE OFFICERS.

Captain.	1st. Lieutenant.	2d. Lieutenant.
A—D. A. LOWBER.	GEO. HURST.	GEO. TEAL.
B—L. D. HARMON.	J. WILLIAMSON.	F. D. POWERS.
C—H. W. BELDEN.	W. G. GREEN.	D. A. SHERWOOD.
D—F. J. MUNGER.	J. RAMSBOTTOM.	J. A. SCOFIELD.
E—W. W. BUCK.	T. EARL.	JOHN SHADBOLT.
F—E. BURNETT.	W. DODGE.	J. W WINCHESTER
G—GEO. GRAHAM.	E. L. DOOLITTLE.	A. A. BABCOCK.
H—F. T. HOBBS.	E. J. GRUMLEY.	J. M. WELLS.
I—GEO. A. BECK.	N. G. ROWLEY.	GEO. L. CROSS.
K—JAS. W HITCHCOCK.	A. J. HOLMES.	N. B. SMITH.

Non-Commissioned Staff.

Prin'l Musician—W. H. BURTON.   *Com. Serg't*— .... CHASE.
Q. M. Serg't—SAM. PICKETT.   *Serg't Major*—H. BABCOCK.
Hospital Steward—PORTER ROUNDY.

L'Envoi.

> The play is done; the curtain drops,
> Slow falling to the prompter's bell,
> A moment yet the actor stops,
> And looks around to bid farewell.
> It is an irksome word and task,
> And when he's laughed and said his say,
> He shews, as he removes his mask,
> A face that's anything but gay.
>
> [*Thackeray.*

My task is almost done, and my pen runs over these few last lines with a feeling closely akin to regret. Regret that this, the last slight tie binding me, as one of their number, to those to whom these pages are dedicated, is broken with their completion; regret at my inability to do better justice to a subject which could well task an abler pen than mine. The labor of its compilation has been trifling and a labor of love. To the whole of my brother officers I return my best thanks for the assistance they have rendered me, both in furnishing me with the official statistics of their companies, and also for their personal reminiscences of scenes we have passed through together, as well as those from which I was absent.

In compiling this history I have, like Othello, simply tried to

—" deliver a round unvarnished tale,"

and while I have tried to do justice to the subject, I have at the same time endeavored not to be tedious; and here

I think of Canning's answer to the clergyman when the latter asked him, "How did you like my sermon? I endeavored not to be tedious," and the statesman tired out by "four heads and an application," wearily responds, "and yet *you were*." At any rate the book goes forth, "with all its imperfections on its head," and if it only serve to while away a dull hour, on some future day, or to call up a kindly memory of the "days of auld lang syne," I shall consider that it has, fully, attained its purpose.

> And whether we shall meet again, I know not,
> Therefore our everlasting farewell take ;
> For ever and for ever fare ye well.
> If we do meet again, why we shall *smile ;*
> If not, why then this parting is well made.
> [*Julius Cæsar.*

And on this the anniversary day of our nation's birth, we sit here in our quiet camp near Washington, overlooking the dome of the Capitol, and the waters of that river by whose side repose the ashes of the Father of his country. The noisy roar of the national salute has long ceased to awaken the echoes of the surrounding hills, the calm quiet of evening is settling down upon us, and as we look round and see the bright stars and stripes of our ensign waving languidly, in the light breeze, over the sleeping engines of war below, our thoughts travel back down the dim, half unreal vista of the months left behind us.

A year ago and treason, with its accompaniments of

bloodshed and devastation, was rampant in the land. A year ago, and we lay on our arms in front of the strongest army, garrisoning one of the strongest fortified places of the whole Confederacy. To-day, that flag that now floats from a hundred places within reach of our vision, floats once more over every State in the Union. To-day the States are once more united—let us hope for ever. To-day we sit here IN PEACE, looking back on our past labors and enjoying their fruits.

> "When the war.drum throbs no longer,
>   And the battle flags are furled
> In the parliament of man,
>   The federation of the world."
>
> [*Tennyson.*

The Rebellion is at an end—the wicked attempt of a few unscrupulous and ambitious politicians to overthrow the freest and best government in the world, has come to naught; and, though a few faint sparks yet smoulder on, the Torch of Secession is quenched. God grant forever.

TENALLYTOWN, D. C., July 4th, 1865.

www.ingramcontent.com/pod-product-compliance
Lightning Source LLC
Chambersburg PA
CBHW020135170426
43199CB00010B/754